PEOPLE'S WAR
PEOPLE'S ARMY

The Viet Công Insurrection Manual
for Underdeveloped Countries

General VO NGUYEN GIAP

PEOPLE'S WAR
PEOPLE'S ARMY

University Press of the Pacific
Honolulu. Hawaii

People's War People's Army

by
General Vo Nguyen Giap

ISBN: 0-89875-371-6

Reprinted from the 1961 edition

University Press of the Pacific
Honolulu, Hawaii
http://www.universitypressofthepacific.com

CONTENTS

ILLUSTRATIONS

HO CHI MINH
President of the Democratic Republic of Viet Nam

CONTENTS

PUBLISHER'S NOTE

We are very pleased to publish the English translation of a series of articles by General Vo Nguyen Giap, member of the Political Bureau of the Central Committee of the Viet Nam Workers' Party, Vice-Prémier and Minister for National Defence of the Democratic Republic of Viet Nam, Commander-in-Chief of the Viet Nam People's Army.

In these articles, the author introduces the liberation war waged by the Vietnamese people, the features of that war, and deals with the reasons for victory: mobilisation of the entire people, setting up of a people's army, merging of all patriotic organisations and people into a united national front, clearsighted leadership of the Party of the working class. It lays particular stress on the problem of organisation and direction of the revolutionary armed forces of Viet Nam. In a word, it is the combination of experiences gained by the Vietnamese people in the course of a long struggle against colonialism, for national independence, struggle which ended in 1954 with the brilliant Dien Bien Phu victory and the signing of the Geneva Agreements.

Publication of this book is most timely.

It is true that since the end of World War II, the maps of Asia, Africa and Latin America have been subject to radical changes, other countries will soon be independent and colonialism is unquestionably doomed to collapse. It is no less true that great obstacles still stand in the way of the peoples struggling for their liberation. The Algerian war has just entered its seventh year. The so-called " U.N. action" in the Congo has turned out to be an imperialist plot against Lumumba's motherland. Cuba is subject to daily provocations by the U.S.A. Half of Viet Nam's territory is still under the heel of a new type colonialism " made in U.S.A. "

We hope that all our friends who, like us, are still suffering from imperialist designs and threats will find in the "People's War, People's Army" what we ourselves have found : further reasons for confidence and hope.

FOREIGN LANGUAGES PUBLISHING HOUSE

THE VIETNAMESE PEOPLE'S WAR OF LIBERATION AGAINST THE FRENCH IMPERIALISTS AND THE AMERICAN INTERVENTIONISTS (1945-1954)

I

A FEW HISTORICAL AND GEOGRAPHICAL CONSIDERATIONS

Viet Nam is one of the oldest countries in South-east Asia.

Stretching like an immense S along the edge of the Pacific, it includes Bac Bo or North Viet Nam which, with the Red River delta, is a region rich in agricultural and industrial possibilities, Nam Bo or South Viet Nam, a vast alluvial plain furrowed by the arms of the Mekong and especially favourable to agriculture, and Trung Bo or Central Viet Nam, a long, narrow belt of land joining them. To describe the shape of their country, the Vietnamese like to recall an image familiar to them : that of a shoulder pole carrying a basket of paddy at each end.

Viet Nam extends over nearly 330.000 square kilometres on which lives a population of approximately 30 million inhabitants. During its many thousands of years old history, the Vietnamese people have always been able to maintain an heroic tradition of struggle against foreign aggression. During the 13th century in particular, they succeeded in thwarting attempts at invasion by the Mongols who had extended their domination over the whole of feudal China.

From the middle of the 19th century, the French imperialists began undertaking the conquest of the country.

Despite resistance lasting dozens of years, Viet Nam was progressively reduced to the state of a colony, thereafter to be integrated in 'French Indo-China' with Cambodia and Laos. But from the first day of French aggression, the national liberation movement of the Vietnamese people unceasingly developed. The repression which attempted to stifle this movement only stirred it up the more; so much so, that after the First World War, it began to take on a powerful mass character and had already won over wide circles of the intellectual and petty bourgeois levels, while penetrating deeply into the peasant masses as well as into the working class which was then beginning to form. The year 1930 saw another step forward with the founding of the Indochinese Communist Party, now the Viet Nam Workers' Party which took upon itself the mission of lead ing the national democratic revolution of the Vietnamese people against the imperialists and the feudal landlord class.

Just after the launching of the Second World War in 1939, France was occupied by the Nazis, while Viet Nam was progressively becoming a colony of the Japanese fascists. The Party was able in good time to appreciate the situation created by this new development. Estimating that a new cycle of war and revolution had begun, it set as a task for the whole nation the widening of the anti-imperialist national united front, the preparation of armed insurrection and the overthrow of the French and Japanese imperialists in order to reconquer national independence. The Viet Nam Doc Lap Dong Minh (League for the Independence of Viet Nam, abbreviated to Viet Minh) was founded and drew in all patriotic classes and social strata. Guerilla warfare was launched in the High Region of Bac Bo. A free zone was formed.

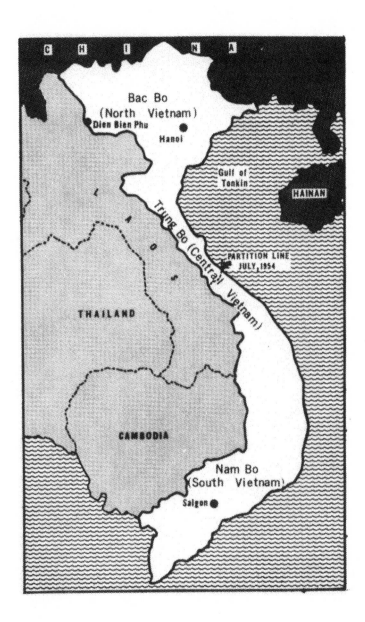

In August 1945, the capitulation of the Japanese forces before the Soviet Army and the Allied forces, put an end to the world war. The defeat of the German and Nippon fascists was the beginning of a great weakening of the capitalist system. After the great victory of the Soviet Union, many people's democracies saw the light of day. The socialist system was no longer confined within the frontiers of a single country. A new historic era was beginning in the world.

In view of these changes, in Viet Nam, the Indo-chinese Communist Party and the Viet Minh called the whole Vietnamese nation to general insurrection. Everywhere, the people rose in a body. Demonstrations and displays of force followed each other uninterruptedly. In August, the Revolution broke out, neutralising the bewildered Nippon troops, overthrowing the pro-Japanese feudal authorities, and installing people's power in Hanoi and throughout the country, in the towns as well as in the countryside, in Bac Bo as well as in Nam Bo. In Hanoi, the capital, in September 2nd, the provisional gouvernment was formed around President Ho Chi Minh ; it presented itself to the nation, proclaimed the independence of Viet Nam, and called on the nation to unite, to hold itself in readiness to defend the country and to oppose all attempts at imperialist aggression. The Democratic Republic of Viet Nam was born, the first people's democracy in South-east Asia.

But the imperialists intended to nip the republican regime in the bud and once again transform Viet Nam into a colony. Three weeks had hardly gone by when, on September 23rd, 1945, the French Expeditionary Corps opened fire in Saigon. The whole Vietnamese nation then rose to resist foreign aggression. From that day, began a war of national liberation which was to be carried on for nine years at the cost of unprecedented heroism and amidst unimaginable difficulties, to end by the shining victory of our people and the crushing defeat of the aggressive imperialists at Dien Bien Phu.

But at a time when, in the amazing enthusiasm aroused by the August Revolution, the Vietnamese people were closing their ranks around the provisional government, a new factor intervened which was to make the political situation more difficult and more complex. According to the terms of an agreement between the Allies, in order to receive the Japanese surrender, the Chinese Kuomintang forces entered in a body in the part of Viet Nam situated north of the 16th parallel, while the British forces landed in the South. The Chiang Kai-shek troop took advantage of the opportunity to pillage the population and sack the country, while using every means to help the most reactionary elements among the Vietnamese bourgeois and landlords — the members of the Viet Nam Quoc Dan Dang (the Vietnamese Kuomintang) and the pro-Japanese Phuc Quoc (Vietnamese National Restoration Party) — to stir up trouble throughout the country. After occupying the five frontier provinces, they provoked incidents even in the capital, and feverishly prepared to overthrow people's power. In the South, the British actively exerted themselves to hasten the return of the French imperialists. Never before had there been so many foreign troops on the soil of Viet Nam. But never before either, had the Vietnamese people been so determined to rise up in combat to defend their country.

These are the broad outlines of the historical and geographical conditions indispensable to an understanding of the unfolding of the war of national liberation of the Vietnamese people.

II

SUMMARY OF THE PROGRESS OF THE
WAR OF NATIONAL LIBERATION

At the outset of the war, the French imperialists' scheme was to rely upon the British troops to reconquer Nam Bo and afterwards to use it as a springboard for preparing their return to the North. They had shamefully capitulated before the Japanese fascists, but after the ending of the world war, they considered the resumption of their place at the head of their former colony as an indisputable right. They refused to admit that in the meantime the situation had radically changed.

In September 1945, French colonial troops armed by the British and soon strengthened by the French Expeditionary Corps under the command of General Leclerc, launched aggression in Saigon, with the direct support of the British army. The population of Nam Bo immediately rose up to fight. In view of the extreme weakness of its forces at the beginning, people's power had to withdraw to the countryside after waging heroic street fights in Saigon and in the large towns. Almost the whole of the towns and important lines of communication in Nam Bo and the South of Trung Bo gradually fell into the hands of the adversary.

The colonialists throught they were on the point of achieving the reconquest of Nam Bo, and General Leclerc declared that occupation and pacification would be completed in ten weeks. But events took quite a different turn. Confident of the support of the whole country, the southern population continued the fight. In all the campaigns in Nam Bo the guerilla forces were going from strength to strength, their bases were being consolidated and extended, and people's power was maintained and strengthened during the nine years of the Resistance, until the re-establishment of peace.

Knowing that the invasion of Nam Bo was only the prelude to a plan of aggression by the French imperialists, our Party guided the whole nation toward preparing a long-term resistance. In order to assemble all the forces against French imperialism, the Party advocated uniting all the elements that could be united, neutralising all those that could be neutralised, and widening the National United Front by the formation of the Lien Viet (Viet Nam People's Front) urgently organising general elections with universal suffrage in order to form the first National Assembly of the Democratic Republic of Viet Nam responsible for passing the Constitution and forming a widely representative resistance government grouping the most diverse elements including even those of the Viet Nam Quoc Dan Dang (the Vietnamese Kuomintang) At that time, we avoided all incidents with the Chiang Kai-shed troops.

The problem then before the French Expeditionary Corps was to know whether it would be easy for them to return to North Viet Nam by force. It was certainly not so, because our forces were more powerful there than in the

South. For its part, our Government intended doing everything in its power to preserve peace so as to enable the newly created people's power to consolidate itself and to rebuild the country devastated by long years of war. It was thus that negotiations which ended in the Preliminary Agreement of March 6 th, 1946, took place between the French colonialists and our Government. According to the terms of this convention, limited contingents of French troops were allowed to station in a certain number of localities in North Viet Nam in order to co-operate with the Vietnamese troops in taking over from the repatriated Chiang Kai-shek forces. In exchange, the French Government recognised Viet Nam as a free state, having its own government, its own national assembly, its own army and finances, and promised to withdraw its troops from Viet Nam within the space of five years. The political status of Nam Bo was to be decided by a referendum.

Relations between the Democratic Republic of Viet Nam and France were then at a crossroads. Would there be a move towards consolidation of peace or a resumption of hostilities? The colonialists considered the Preliminary Agreement as a provisional expedient enabling them to introduce part of their troops into the North of Viet Nam, a delaying stratagem for preparing the war they intended to continue. Therefore, the talks at the Dalat Conference led to no result and those at the Fontainebleau Conference resulted only in the signing of an unstable modus vivendi. During the whole of this time, the colonialists partisans of war were steadily pursuing their tactics of local encroachments. Instead of observing the armistice, they continued their mopping-up operations in Nam Bo, and set up a local puppet government there ; in Bac Bo they increased provocations and attacked a certain number of provinces, pillaging and massacring the population of the Hongai mining area, and everywhere creating an atmosphere of tension preparatory to attacks by force.

Loyal to its policy of peace and independence, our Government vainly endeavoured to settle conflicts in a friendly manner, many times appealing to the French Government then presided over by the S.F.I.O. (Socialist Party) to change their policy in order to avoid a war detrimental to both sides. At the same time we busied ourselves with strengthening our rear with a view to resistance. We obtained good results in intensifying production. We paid much attention to strengthening national defence. The liquidating of the reactionaries of the Viet Nam Quoc Dan Dang was crowned with success and we were able to liberate all the areas which had fallen into their hands.

In November 1946, the situation worsened. The colonialists by a *coup de force* in Haiphong seized the town. After engaging in street fights, our troops withdrew to the suburbs. In December, the colonialists provoked tension in Hanoi, massacred civilians, seized a number of public offices, sent an ultimatum demanding the disarming of our self-defence groups and the right to ensure order in the town, and finally provoked armed conflict. Obstinately the colonialists chose war, which led to their ruin.

On December 19th, resistance broke out throughout the country. The next day, in the name of the Party and of the Government, President Ho Chi Minh called on the whole people to rise up to exterminate the enemy and save the country, to fight to the last drop of blood, and whatever the cost, to refuse re-enslavement.

* * *

At the time when hostilities became generalised throughout the country, what was the balance of forces? From the point of view of material, the enemy was stronger than us. Our troops were thus ordered to fight the enemy wherever they were garrisoned so as to weaken them and prevent them spreading out too rapidly, and thereafter, when conditions became unfavourable to us, to make the bulk of our forces fall back towards our rear in order to keep our forces intact with a view to a long-term resistance. The most glorious and most remarkable combats took place in Hanoi, where our troops succeeded in firmly holding a huge sector for two months before with-drawing from the capital unhurt.

The whole Vietnamese people remained indissolubly united in a fight to the death in those days when the country was in danger. Replying to the appeal by the Party, they resolutely chose the path of Freedom and Independence. The central government, having withdrawn to bases in the mountainous region of Viet Bac, military zones — soon united in interzones — were formed, and the power of local authorities was strengthened for mobilising the whole people and organising the resistance. Our government continued appealing to the Frenh government not to persist in their error and to reopen peaceful negotiations. But the latter under the pretext of negotiation demanded the disarming of our troops. We replied to the colonialists' obstinacy by intensifying the resistance.

In fact, the French High Command began regrouping forces to prepare a fairly big lightning offensive in the hope of ending the war. In October 1947, they launched a big campaign against our principal base, Viet Bac, in order to annihilate the nerve centre of the resistance and destroy

19

our regular forces. But this large-scale operation ended in a crushing defeat. The forces of the Expeditionary Corps suffered heavy losses without succeeding in causing anxiety to our leading organisations or impairing our regular units. It was a blow to the enemy's strategy of a lightning war and a rapid solution. Our people were all the more determined to persevere along the path of a long-term resistance.

* * *

From 1948, realising that the war was prolonging itself, the enemy changed their strategy. They used the main part of their forces for "pacification" and for consolidating the already occupied areas, in Nam Bo especially, applying the principle : fight Vietnamese with Vietnamese, feed war with war. They set up a puppet central government, actively organised supplementary local units, and indulged in economic pillage. They gradually extended their zone of occupation in the North and placed under their control the major part of the Red River delta. During all these years, the French Expeditionary Corps followed a procedure of great dispersion, scattering their forces in thousands of military posts to occupy territory and control the localities. But ever-growing military and financial difficulties gradually led the French imperialists to let the American imperialists interfere in the conflict.

* * *

The enemy having altered their strategy, we then advocated the wide development of guerilla warfare, transforming the former's rear into our front line. Our units operated in small pockets, with independent companies penetrating deeply into the enemy-controlled zone to launch guerilla warfare, establish bases and protect local people's power. It was an extremely hard war generalised in all domains: military, economic and political. The enemy mopped-up, we fought against mopping-up. They organised supplementary local Vietnamese troops and installed puppet authorities; we firmly upheld local people's power, overthrew men of straw, eliminated traitors and carried out active propaganda to bring about the disintegration of the supplementary forces. We gradually formed a network of guerilla bases. On the map showing the theatre of operations besides the free zone, "red zones", which ceaselessly spread and multiplied, began to appear right in the heart of the occupied areas. The soil of the fatherland was being freed inch by inch right in the enemy's rear lines. There was no clearly-defined front in this war. It was there where the enemy was. The front was nowhere, it was everywhere. Our new strategy created serious difficulties for the enemy's plan to feed war with war and to fight Vietnamese with Vietnamese and finally brought about their defeat.

The centre of gravity of the front was gradually moving towards the enemy's rear. During this time, the free zone was continually being consolidated. Our army was growing in the struggle. The more our guerillas developed and the more our local units grew, the more we found ourselves able to regroup our forces. At the end of 1948 and the beginning of 1949, for the first time we launched small campaigns which inflicted considerable losses on our adversary. The imperialists were beginning to feel great anxiety. The commission of enquiry presided over by General Revers made a fairly pessimistic report which came to the conclusion that it was necessary to ask the United States for more aid.

* * *

1949 saw the brilliant triumph of the Chinese Revolution and the birth of the People's Republic of China. This great historic event which altered events in Asia and the world, exerted a considerable influence on the war of liberation of the Vietnamese people. Viet Nam was no longer in the grip of enemy encirclement, and was henceforth geographically linked to the socialist bloc.

At the beginning of 1950, the Democratic Republic of Viet Nam was officially recognised by the People's Republic of China, the Soviet Union and the brother countries. The following year, the second Congress of the Indochinese Communist Party decided to alter the name of the Party and founded the Viet Nam Workers' Party. The Viet Minh and the Lien Viet were amalgamated. In 1953, the Party and the Government decided to carry out agrarian reform in order to liberate productive forces and give a more vigorous impulse to the Resistance. All these facts contributed to shaping to our advantage the course of our struggle.

In effect, 1950 marked the opening of a new phase in the evolution of our long Resistance. During the winter, in the frontier campaign, for the first time, we opened a relatively big counter-attack which resulted in the liberation of the provinces of Cao Bang, Lang Son and Lao Cai. Immediately after, we began a series of offensive operations on the delta front.

The enemy, routed, sent General De Lattre de Tassigny to Indo-China. The military aid granted by the United States following an agreement signed in 1950, was on the increase. The aggressive war waged by the French colonialists gradually became a war carried out with "U.S. dollars" and "French blood". It was really a 'dirty war'.

De Lattre's plan, approved by Washington, provided for a strong line of bunkers in the Red River delta to stop our progress, and for a regrouping of forces in order to launch violent mopping-up operations so as at all costs to 'pacify' the rear and create the right conditions for an offensive which would enable the French forces to recapture the initiative while attacking our free zone. In October 1951, the enemy occupied Hoa Binh. We replied by immediately launching the Hoa Binh campaign. On the one hand we contained and overwhelmed the adversary's forces on the "opposite" front, on the other hand, we took advantage of their exposed disposition of troops to get our divisions to strike direct blows at their rear in the Red River delta. Our large guerilla bases were extending further still, freeing nearly two million inhabitants. Hoa Binh was released. De Lattre's plan was checked.

In 1952, we launched a campaign in the North-Western zone and freed vast territories as far as Dien Bien Phu. At the beginning of 1953, units of Vietnamese volunteers, co-operating with the Pathet Lao liberation army, began the campaign in Higher Laos which brought about the liberation of Sam Neua.

In short, the face of the various theatres of operations was as follows:

The main front was that of North Viet Nam where most of the big battles were taking place. At the beginning of 1953, almost the whole of the mountainous region, say, more than two thirds of the territory of North Viet Nam, had been liberated. The enemy still occupied Hanoi and the

Red River delta, but outside the large towns and the important lines of communication, our enlarged guerilla bases—our free zone — already embraced nearly two thirds of the villages and localities situated in the enemy rear. In Central and South Viet Nam, we still firmly held vast free zones while continuing powerfully to develop our guerilla bases in the occupied zone.

The face of the theatres of operations had greatly altered : the zone of enemy occupation had been gradually reduced, whereas the main base of the Resistance — the free zone of North Viet Nam, had gone on extending and being consolidated day by day. Our forces constantly maintained the initiative in operations. The enemy found themselves driven into a very dangerous impasse.

The French imperialists were getting more and more bogged down in their unjust war of aggression. American aid, which covered 15 per cent of the expenditure on this war in 1950 and 1951, rose to 35 per cent in 1952, 45 per cent in 1953, soon to reach 80 per cent in 1954 But the situation of the French Expeditionary Corps remained without much hope. In Autumn 1953, taking advantage of the armistice in Korea, the American and French imperialists plotted to increase their armed forces in Indo-China in the hope of prolonging and extending hostilities.

They decided on the Navarre plan which proposed to crush the main part of our forces, to occupy the whole of Viet nam, to transform it into a colony and a Franco-American military base and to end the war victoriously within 18 months. It was, in fact, the plan of the " war-to-the-end " men, Laniel and Dulles. In order to realise the first phase of this plan, General Navarre assembled in the North more than half the entire mobile forces of the Indochinese theatre, including reinforcements newly arrived from France, launched attacks against our free zone, and parachuted troops into Dien Bien Phu to turn it into the springboard for a future offensive.

* *

The enemy wanted to concentrate their forces. We compelled them to disperse. By successively launching strong offensives on the points they had left relatively unprotected, we obliged them to scatter their troops all over the place in order to ward off our blows, and thus created favourable conditions for the attack at Dien Bien Phu, the most powerful entrenched camp in Indo-China, considered invulnerable by the Franco-American general staff. We decided to take the enemy by the throat at Dien Bien Phu. The major part of our forces were concentrated there. We mobilised the entire potentiality of the population of the free zone in order to guarantee victory for our front line. After 55 days and 55 nights of fighting, the Viet Nam People's Army accomplished the greatest feat of arms of the whole war of liberation: the entire garrison at Dien Bien Phu was annihilated. This great campaign, which altered the course of the war, contributed decisively to the success of the Geneva Conference.

In July 1954, the signing of the Geneva Agreements re-established peace in Indo-China on the basis of respect for the sovereignty, independence, unity and territorial integrity of Viet Nam, Cambodia and Laos. It is following these agreements that North Viet Nam, with a population of 16 million inhabitants, is today entirely free. This success crowned nearly a century of struggle for national liberation, and especially the nine long and hard years of resistance war waged by the Vietnamese people. It was a crushing defeat for the French and American imperialists as well as for their lackeys. But at present, half of our country is still living under the yoke of the American imperialists and the Ngo Dinh Diem authorities. Our people's struggle for national liberation is not yet finished, it is continuing by peaceful means.

III

THE FUNDAMENTAL PROBLEMS OF
OUR WAR OF LIBERATION

The Vietnamese people's war of liberation was a just war, aiming to win back the independence and unity of the country, to bring land to our peasants and guarantee them the right to it, and to defend the achievements of the August Revolution. That is why it was first and foremost a *people's war*. To educate, mobilise, organise and arm the whole people in order that they might take part in the Resistance was a crucial question.

The enemy of the Vietnamese nation was aggressive imperialism, which had to be overthrown. But the latter having long since joined up with the feudal landlords, the anti-imperialist struggle could definitely not be separated from anti-feudal action. On the other hand, in a backward colonial country such as ours where the peasants make up the majority of the population, a people's war is essentially *a peasant's war under the leadership of the working class*. Owing to this fact, a general mobilisation of the whole people is neither more nor less than the mobilisation of the rural masses. The problem of land is of decisive importance. From an exhaustive analysis, the Vietnamese people's war of liberation was essentially a people's national democratic revolution carried out under armed form and had twofold fundamental task: the overthrowing of imperialism and the defeat of the feudal landlord class, the anti-imperialist struggle being the primary task.

A backward colonial country which had only just risen up to proclaim its independence and install people's power, Viet Nam only recently possessed armed forces, equipped with still very mediocre arms and having no combat experience. Her enemy, on the other hand, was an imperialist power which has retained a fairly considerable economic and military potentiality despite the recent German occupation and benefited, furthermore, from the active support of the United States. The balance of forces decidedly showed up our weaknesses against the enemy's power. The Vietnamese people's war of liberation had, therefore, to be a hard and long-lasting war in order to succeed in creating conditions for victory. All the conceptions born of impatience and aimed at obtaining speedy victory could only be gross errors. It was necessary to firmly grasp the strategy of a long-term resistance, and to exalt the will to be self-supporting in order to maintain and gradually augment our forces, while nibbling at and progressively destroying those of the enemy; it was necessary to accumulate thousands of small victories to turn them into a great success, thus gradually altering the balance of forces, in transforming our weakness into power and carrying off final victory

At an early stage, our Party was able to discern the characteristics of this war: a people's war and a long-lasting war, and it was by proceeding from these premises that, during the whole of hostilities and in particularly difficult conditions, the Party solved all the problems of the Resistance. This judicious leadership by the Party led us to victory.

*
* *

From the point of view of directing operations, our *strategy and tactics had to be those of a people's war and of a long-term resistance.*

Our strategy was, as we have stressed, to wage a long-lasting battle. A war of this nature in general entails several phases; in principle, starting from a stage of contention, it goes through a period of equilibrium before arriving at a general counter-offensive. In effect, the way in which it is carried on can be more subtle and more complex, depending on the particular conditions obtaining on both sides during the course of operations. Only a long-term war could enable us to utilise to the maximum our political trump cards, to overcome our material handicap and to transform our weakness into strength. To maintain and increase our forces, was the principle to which we adhered, contenting ourselves with attacking when success was certain, refusing to give battle likely to incur losses to us or to engage in hazardous actions. We had to apply the slogan : to build up our strength during the actual course of fighting.

The forms of fighting had to be completely adapted that is, to raise the fighting spirit to the maximum and rely on heroism of our troops to overcome the enemy's material superiority. In the main, especially at the outset of the war, we had recourse to guerilla fighting. In the Vietnamese theatre of operations, this method carried off great victories: it could be used in the mountains as well as in the delta, it could be waged with good or mediocre material and even without arms, and was to enable us eventually to equip ourselves at the cost of the enemy. Wherever the Expeditionary Corps came, the entire population took part in the fighting ; every commune had its fortified village, every district had its regional troops fighting under the command of the local branches of the Party and the people's administration, in liaison with the regular forces in order to wear down and annihilate the enemy forces.

Thereafter, with the development of our forces, guerilla warfare changed into a mobile warfare — a form of mobile warfare still strongly marked by guerilla warfare — which would afterwards become the essential form of operations on the main front, the northern front. In this process of development of guerilla warfare and of accentuation of the mobile warfare, our people's army constantly grew and passed from the stage of combats involving a section or company, to fairly large-scale campaigns bringing into action several divisions. Gradually, its equipment improved, mainly by the seizure of arms from the enemy — the material of the French and American imperialists.

From the military point of view, *the Vietnamese people's war of liberation proved that an insufficiently equipped people's army, but an army fighting for a just cause, can, with appropriate strategy and tactics, combine the conditions needed to conquer a modern army of aggressive imperialism.*

* *

Concerning the management of a war economy within the framework of an agriculturally backward country undertaking a long-term resistance as was the case in Viet Nam, the problem of the rear lines arose under the form of building resistance bases in the countryside. The raising and defence of production, and the development of agriculture, were problems of great importance for supplying the front as well as for the progressive improvement of the people's living conditions. The question of manufacturing arms was not one which could be set aside.

In the building of rural bases and the reinforcement of the rear lines for giving an impulse to the resistance, the agrarian policy of the Party played a determining role. Therein lay the anti-feudal task of the revolution. In a colony where the national question is essentially the peasant question, the consolidation of the resistance forces was possible only by a solution to the agrarian problem.

The August Revolution overthrew the feudal State. The reduction of land rents and rates of interest decreed by people's power bestowed on the peasants their first material advantages. Land monopolised by the imperialists and the traitors was confiscated and shared out. Communal land and ricefields were more equitably distributed. From 1953, deeming it necessary to promote the accomplishment of anti-feudal tasks, the Party decided to achieve agrarian reform even during the course of the resistance war. Despite the errors which blemished its accomplishment, it was a correct line crowned with success; it resulted in real material advantages for the peasants and brought to the army and the people a new breath of enthusiasm in the war of resistance

Thanks to this just agrarian policy, the life of the people, in the hardest conditions of the resistance war, in general improved, not only in the wast free zones of the North, but even in the guerilla bases in South Viet Nam.

The Vietnamese people's war of liberation brought out the importance of building resistance bases in the countryside and the close and indissoluble relationships between the anti-imperialist revolution and the anti-feudal revolution.

From the political point of view, the question of unity among the people and the mobilisation of all energies in the war of resistance were of paramount importance. It was at the same time a question of the national united front against the imperialists and their lackeys, the Vietnamese traitors.

In Viet Nam, our Party carried off a great success in its policy of Front. As early as during the difficult days of the Second World War, it formed the League for the Independence of Viet Nam. At the time of and during the early years of the war of resistance, it postponed the application of its watchwords on the agrarian revolution, limiting its programme to the reduction of land rents and interest rates, which enabled us to neutralise part of the landlord class and to rally around us the most patriotic of them.

From the early days of the August Revolution, the policy of broad front adopted by the Party neutralised the wavering elements among the landlord class and limited the acts of sabotage by the partisans of the Viet Nam Quoc Dan Dang.

Thereafter, in the course of development of the resistance war, when agrarian reform had become an urgent necessity, our Party applied itself to making a differentiation within the bosom of the landlord class by providing in its political line for different treatment for each type of landlord according to the latter's political attitude, on the principle of liquidation of the regime of feudal appropriation of land.

The policy of unity among nationalities adopted by the National United Front also achieved great successes and the programme of unity with the various religious circles attained good results.

The National United Front was to be a vast assembly of all the forces capable of being united, neutralising all those which could be neutralised, dividing all those it was possible to divide in order to direct the spearhead at the chief enemy of the revolution, invading imperialism. It was to be established on the basis of an alliance between workers and peasants and placed under the leadership of the working class. In Viet Nam, the question of an alliance between workers and peasants was backed by a dazzling history and firm traditions, the party of the working class having been the only political party to fight resolutely in all circumstances for national independence, and the first to put forward the watchword " land to the tillers " and to struggle determinedly for its realisation. However, in the early years of the resistance a certain under-estimation of the importance of the peasant question hindered us from giving all the necessary attention to the worker-peasant alliance. This error was subsequently put right, especially from the moment when the Party decided, by means of accomplishing agrarian reform, to make the peasants the real masters of the countryside. At present, after the victory of the resistance and of agrarian reform, when the Party has restored independence to half the country and brought land to the peasants, the bases of the worker-peasant alliance will daily go from strength to strength.

The war of liberation of the Vietnamese people proves that, in the face of an enemy as powerful as he is cruel, victory is possible only by uniting the whole people within the bosom of a firm and wide national united front based on the worker-peasant alliance.

IV

THE FACTORS OF SUCCESS

The Vietnamese people's war of liberation has won great victories. In North Viet Nam, entirely freed, the imperialist enemy has been overthrown, the landlords have been got rid of as a class, and the population is advancing with a firm tread on the path of building socialism to make of the North a firm base of action for the reunification of the country.

The Vietnamese people's war of liberation was victorious because it was a just war, waged for independence and the reunification of the country, in the legitimate interests of the nation and the people and which by this fact succeeded in leading the whole people to participate enthusiastically in the resistance and to consent to make every sacrifice for its victory.

The Vietnamese people's war of liberation won this great victory because we had a revolutionary armed force of the people, the *heroic Viet Nam People's Army*. Built in accordance with the political line of the Party, this army was animated by an unflinching combative spirit, and accustomed to a style of persevering political work. It adopted the tactics and strategy of a people's war. It developed from nothing by combining the best elements among the workers, peasants and revolutionary students and intellectuals, stemming from the patriotic organisations of the popular masses. Born of the people, it fought for the people. It is an army led by the Party of the working class.

The Vietnamese people's war of liberation was victorious because we had a wide and firm *National United Front*, comprising all the revolutionary classes, all the nationalities living on Vietnamese soil, all the patriots. This Front was based on the alliance between workers and peasants, under the leadership of the Party.

The Vietnamese people's war of liberation ended in victory because of the existence of *people's power* established during the August Revolution and thereafter constantly consolidated. This power was the Government of alliance between classes, the government of the revolutionary classes and above all of the workers and peasants. It was the dictatorship of people's democracy, the dictatorship of the workers and peasants in fact, under the leadership of the Party. It devoted its efforts to mobilising and organising the whole people for the Resistance; it brought the people material advantages not only in the free zones, but also in the guerilla bases behind the enemy's back.

The Vietnamese people's war of liberation attained this great victory for the reasons we have just enumerated, but above all because it was *organised and led by the Party of the working class: the Indochinese Communist Party, now the Viet Nam Workers' Party.* In the light of the principles of Marxism-Leninism, it was this Party which proceeded to make an analysis of the social situation and of the balance of forces between the enemy and ourselves in order to determine the fundamental tasks of the people's national democratic revolution, to establish the plan for the armed struggle and decide on the guiding principle: long-term resistance and self-reliance. It was the Party which found a correct solution to the problems arising out of the setting up and leadership of a people's army, people's power and a national united front. It also inspired in the people and the army a completely revolutionary spirit which instilled into the whole people the will to overcome all difficulties, to endure all privations, the spirit of a long resistance, of resistance to the end. Our Party, under the leadership of President Ho Chi Minh, is the worthy Party of the working class and the nation. President Ho Chi Minh, leader of the Party and the nation, is the symbol of this gigantic uprising of the Vietnamese people.

If the Vietnamese people's war of liberation ended in a glorious victory, it is because we did not fight alone, but with the *support of progressive peoples the world over, and more especially the peoples of the brother countries, with the Soviet Union at the head*. The victory of the Vietnamese people cannot be divided from this support; it cannot be disassociated from the brilliant successes of the socialist countries and the movement of national liberation, neither can it be detached from the victories of the Soviet Red Army during the Second World War, nor from those of the Chinese people during the last few years. It cannot be isolated from the sympathy and support of progressive peoples throughout the world, among whom are the French people under the leadership of their Communist Party, and the peoples of Asia and Africa.

The victory of the Vietnamese people is that of a small and weak nation and possessing no regular army, which rose up to engage in an armed struggle against the aggression of an imperialist country with a modern army and benefiting from the support of the American imperialists. This colonial country has established and maintained a regime of people's democracy, which will open up to it the path to socialism. That is one of the great historic events in the national liberation movement and in the proletarian revolutionary movement, in the new international position born of the Second World War, in the period of transition from capitalism to socialism, in the time of the disintegration of imperialism. The Vietnamese people's war of liberation has contributed to making obvious this new historic truth: in the present international situation, a weak people which rises up resolutely to fight for its freedom is sure to triumph over all enemies and to achieve victory.

This great truth enlightens and encourages the Vietnamese people on the path of struggle for peace, socialism and the reunification of the country. This path will certainly lead it to new victories.

General Vo Nguyen Giap

PEOPLE'S WAR
PEOPLE'S ARMY

*Article written on the occasion of the XVth
anniversary of the Viet Nam People's Army*

On December 22, 1959, the Viet Nam People's Army will celebrate the fifteenth anniversary of its founding. I would like, on this occasion to have a few words with you about the struggle and the building up of the revolutionary armed forces in Viet Nam. At the same time I would like to lay emphasis on the fundamental points which bring out the characteristics of the military policy of the vanguard party of the Vietnamese working class and people — the Indochinese Communist Party—now the Viet Nam Workers' Party.

As Marxism-Leninism teaches us : " The history of all societies up till the present day, bas been but the history of class struggle. " These struggles can take either the form of political struggle or the form of armed struggle — the armed struggle being only the continuation of the political struggle. In a society which remains divided into classes, we can distinguish two kinds of politics : the politics of the classes and nations of exploiters and oppressors and that of the exploited and oppressed classes and nations. Hence two kinds of wars, of States and armies diametrically opposed to each other, the ones revolutionary, popular and just, and the others counter-revolutionary, anti-popular and unjust.

The Russian October Revolution marked a new era in the history of mankind. A state of a new type appeared, that of proletarian dictatorship, that of the liberated Soviet workers and peasants, toiling people and nationalities. An army of a new type came into being — the Red Army, a genuine people's army placed under the leadership of the Communist Party of the Soviet Union. Born in the October uprising, and steeled and tempered in the combats that followed it, the Red Army was to become, in a short time, the most powerful army in the world, always ready to defend the Soviet Motherland, the first State of workers and peasants.

In Asia, after World War One, the national democratic revolution of the Chinese people made tremendous progress under the good influence of the Russian Revolution. To free themselves, the Chinese people valiantly rose to wage an armed struggle for many decades. It was in this revolutionary war full of heroism and sacrifices that was born and grew up the Chinese Liberation Army, an army equally of a new type, genuinely popular, under the leadership of the Chinese Communist Party.

Only fifteen years of age, the Viet Nam People's Army is a young revolutionary army. It developed in the course of the national liberation war of the Vietnamese people from which it comes, and is now assuming the glorious task of defending the building of socialism in the North while contributing to make it a strong base for the peaceful reunification of the country. It also constitutes an army of a new type, a truly popular army under the leadership of the working class Party of Viet Nam.

In the U.S.S.R. as well as in China and Viet Nam, the revolutionary wars and armies have common fundamental characteristics : their popular and revolutionary nature, and the just cause they serve.

The Vietnamese revolutionary war and army however have their own characteristics. Indeed, from the very start, in the Soviet Union, the revolutionary war evolved within the framework of a socialist revolution. Moreover it proceeded in an independent country possessing a fairly important modern industrial economy, which, under the socialist regime, has not ceased to develop further. As for the revolutionary war in China, it remained for a long period within the framework of a national democratic revolution proceeding in a semi-colonial country, an immensely vast country and with a population of more than 600 million people.

The revolutionary war in Viet Nam, while advancing as in China towards the objectives of a national democratic revolution, differs for the reason that it took place in a colonial country, in a much smaller country than China in both area and population.

Therefore the history of the armed struggle and the building up of the armed forces in Viet Nam is that of a small nation subject to colonial rule and having neither a vast territory nor a large population, which, though lacking a regular army at the beginning, had to rise against the aggressive forces of an imperialist power, and triumphed over them in the end, liberating half of the country and enabling it to embark on the socialist path. As for the military policy of the vanguard Party of the Vietnamese working class, it is an application of Marxism-Leninism to the concrete conditions of the war of liberation in a colonial country.

I

Viet Nam is a nation in South-east Asia with a very old history. With its 329,600 square kilometres and 30 million inhabitants and its geographical situation in the Pacific, it has now become one of the outposts of the socialist world.

In the course of its thousands of years of history, many a time, the Vietnamese nation victoriously resisted the invasions of the Chinese feudalists. It can be proud of its traditions of undaunted struggle in safeguarding national independence.

After its invasion of Viet Nam in the second half of the 19th century, French imperialism made it their colony. Since then, the struggle against French colonialism never ceased to extend, uprisings succeeded each other in spite of repression, and daily attracting wider and wider strata belonging to all social classes.

In 1930, the Indochinese Communist Party was founded. Under its firm and clear-sighted leadership, the movement for national liberation of the Vietnamese people made new progress. After ten years of heroic political struggle, at the dawn of World War Two, the Party advocated the preparation for armed struggle, and for that the launching of a guerilla war and the setting up of a free zone. The anti-Japanese movement for national salvation, in its irresistible upsurge, led to the glorious days of the August Revolution of 1945. Taking advantage of the major events in the international situation at the time — the victory of the Soviet Red Army and Allied forces over Japanese fascism — the Vietnamese people rose up as one man in the victorious insurrection and set up the people's power. The Democratic Republic of Viet Nam was born, the first people's democracy in South-east Asia.

The political situation in Viet Nam was then particularly difficult and complicated. Chiang Kai-shek's troops had entered the North, and those of Great Britain the South of the country, to disarm the Japanese who were still in possession of all their armaments in the first days of the capitulation. It was in these conditions that French imperialists, immediately after the founding of the Democratic Republic, unleashed a war of reconquest against Viet Nam hoping to impose their domination on this country.

In response to the appeal of the Party and the Government headed by President Ho Chi Minh, the Vietnamese people rose up as one man for the defence of the Fatherland. A sacred war for national liberation began. All hopes of a peaceful settlement were not lost however. A Preliminary Agreement for the cessation of hostilities was signed in March 1946 between the Government of the Democratic Republic of Viet Nam and that of France. But the French colonialists saw it only as a delaying scheme. Therefore, immediately after the signing of the Agreement, they shamelessly violated it by successively occupying various regions. In December 1946, the war spread to the whole country. It was to rage for nine years, nine years after the end of World War Two. And it ended with the brilliant victory of the Vietnamese people.

Our war of liberation was a *people's war*, a just war. It was this essential characteristic that was to determine its laws and to decide its final outcome.

At the first gun-shots of the imperialist invasion, general Leclerc, the first Commander of the French Expeditionary Corps estimated that the operation for the reoccupation of Viet Nam would be a mere military walk over. When encountering the resistance of the Vietnamese people in the South the French generals considered it as weak and temporary and stuck to their opinion that it would take them ten weeks at the most to occupy and pacify the whole of south Viet Nam. Why did French colonialists make such an estimation? Because they considered that to meet their aggression, there must be an army. The Vietnamese army had just been created. It was still numerically weak, badly organised, led by inexperienced officers and non-commissioned officers, provided with old and insufficient equipment, a very limited stock of munitions and having neither tanks, airplanes nor artillery. With such an army how could serious resistance be undertaken and the attacks of the powerful and armoured division repelled? All it could do was to use up its stock of munitions before laying down its arms. In fact, the Vietnamese army was then weak in all respects and was destitute of everything. French colonialists were right in this respect. But is was not possible for them to understand a fundamental and decisive fact : this fact was that the Vietnamese army, though very weak materially was a people's army. This fact is that the war in Viet nam was not only the opposition of two armies. In provoking hostilities, the aggressive colonialists had alienated a whole nation. And, indeed, the whole Vietnamese nation, the entire Vietnamese people rose against them. Unable to grasp this profound truth, the French generals who believed in an easy victory, went instead to certain defeat. They thought they could easily subdue the Vietnamese people, when, in fact, the latter were going to smash them.

Even to this day bourgeois strategists have not yet overcome their surprise at the outcome of the war in Indo-China. How could the Vietnamese nation have defeated an imperialist power such as France which was backed by the U.S.? They try to explain this extraordinary fact by the correctness of strategy and tactics, by the forms of combat and the heroism of the Viet Nam People's Army. Of course all these factors contributed to the happy outcome of the resistance. But if the question is put: " Why were the Vietnamese people able to win? " the most precise and most complete answer must be: " The Vietnamese people won because their war of liberation was a people's war."

When the Resistance War spread to the whole country, the Indochinese Communist Party emphasized in its instructions that our Resistance War must be the work of the entire people. Therein lies the key to victory.

Our Resistance War was a people's war, because its political aims were to smash the imperialist yoke to win back national independence, to overthrow the feudal land-lord class to bring land to the peasants; in other words, to radically solve the two fundamental contradictions of Vietnamese society — contradiction between the nation and imperialism on the one hand, and contradiction between the people, especially between the peasants and the feudal landlord class on the other—and to pave the socialist path for the Vietnamese revolution.

Holding firmly to the strategy and tactics of the national democratic revolution, the Party pointed out to the people the aims of the struggle: independence and democracy. It was, however, not enough to have objectives entirely in conformity with the fundamental aspirations of the people. It was also necessary to bring everything into play to enlighten the masses of the people, educate and encourage them, organise them in fighting for national salvation. The Party devoted itself entirely to this work, to the regrouping of all the national forces, and to the broadening and strengthening of a national united front, the Viet Minh, and later the Lien Viet which was a magnificent model of the unity of the various strata of the people in the anti-imperialist struggle in a colonial country. In fact, this front united the patriotic forces of all classes and social strata, even progressive landlords; all nationalities in the country — majority as well as minority; patriotic believers of each and every religion. " Unity, the great unity, for victory, the great victory "; this slogan launched by President Ho Chi Minh became a reality, a great reality during the long and hard resistance.

We waged a people's war, and that in the framework of a long since colonised country. Therefore the national factor was of first importance. We had to rally all the forces likely to overthrow the imperialists and their lackeys. On the other hand, this war proceeded in a backward agricultural country where the peasants, making up the great majority of the population, constituted the essential force of the revolution and of the Resistance War. Consequently the relation between the national question and the peasant question had to be clearly defined, with the gradual settlement of the agrarian problem, so as to mobilise the broad peasant masses, one of the essential and decisive factors for victory. Always solicitous about the interests of the peasantry, the Party began by advocating reduction of land rent and interest. Later on, as soon as the stabilisation of the situation allowed it, the Party carried out with great firmness the mobilisation of the masses for land reform in order to bring land to the tillers, thereby to maintain and strengthen the Resistance.

During the years of war, various erroneous tendencies appeared. Either we devoted our attention only to the organisation and growth of the armed forces while neglecting the mobilisation and organisation of large strata of the people, or we mobilised the people for the war without heeding seriously their immediate everyday interests ; or we thought of satisfying the immediate interests of the people as a whole, without giving due attention to those of the peasants. The Party resolutely fought all these tendencies. To lead the Resistance to victory, we had to look after the strengthening of the army, while giving thought to mobilising and educating the people, broadening and consolidating the National United Front. We had to mobilise the masses for the Resistance while trying to satisfy their immediate interests to improve their living conditions, essentially those of the peasantry. A very broad national united front was indispensable, on the basis of the worker-peasant alliance and under the leadership of the Party.

* * *

The imperatives of the people's war in Viet Nam required the adoption of appropriate strategy and tactics, on the basis of the enemy's characteristics and of our own, of the concrete conditions of the battlefields and balance of forces facing each other. In other words, the strategy and tactics of a people's war, in an economically backward, colonial country.

First of all, this strategy must be the *strategy of a long-term war*. It does not mean that all revolutionary wars, all people's wars must necessarily be long-term wars. If from the outset, the conditions are favourable to the people and the balance of forces turn in favour of the revolution, the revolutionary war can end victoriously in a short time. But the war of· liberation of the Vietnamese people started in quite different conditions : We had to deal with a much stronger enemy. It was patent that this balance of forces took away from us the possibility of giving decisive battles from the opening of the hostilities and of checking the aggression from the first landing operations on our soil. In a word, it was impossible for us to defeat the enemy swiftly.

It was only by a long and hard resistance that we could wear out the enemy forces little by little while strengthening ours, progressively turn the balance of forces in our favour and finally win victory. We did not have any other way.

This strategy and slogan of long term resistance was decided upon by the Indochinese Communist Party from the first days of the war of liberation. It was in this spirit that the Viet Nam People's Army, after fierce street-combats in the big cities, beat strategical retreats to the countryside on its own initiative in order to maintain its bases and preserve its forces.

The long-term revolutionary war must include several different stages : stage of contention, stage of equilibrium and stage of counter-offensive. Practical fighting was, of course, more complicated. There had to be many years of more and more intense and generalised guerilla fighting to realise the equilibrium of forces and develop our war potentiality. When the conjunctures of events at home and abroad allowed it, we went over to counter-offensive first by a series of local operations then by others on a larger scale which were to lead to the decisive victory of Dien Bien Phu.

The application of this strategy of long-term resistance required a whole system of education, a whole ideological struggle among the people and Party members, a gigantic effort of organisation in both military and economic fields, extraordinary sacrifices and heroism from the army as well as from the people, at the front as well as in the rear. Sometimes erroneous tendencies appeared, trying either to by-pass the stages to end the war earlier, or to throw important forces into military adventures. The Party rectified them by a stubborn struggle and persevered in the line it had fixed. In the difficult hours, certain hesitations revealed themselves, the Party faced them with vigour and with determination in the struggle and faith in final victory.

* * *

The long-term people's war in Viet Nam also called for appropriate forms of fighting: appropriate to the revolutionary nature of the war as well as to the balance of forces which revealed at that time an overwhelming superiority of the enemy over the still very weak material and technical bases of the People's Army. *The adopted form of fighting was guerilla warfare.* It can be said that the war of liberation of the Vietnamese people was a long and vast guerilla war proceeding from simple to complex then to mobile war in the last years of the Resistance.

Guerilla war is the war of the broad masses of an economically backward country standing up against a powerfully equipped and well trained army of aggression. Is the enemy strong? One avoids him. Is he weak? One attacks him. To his modern armament one opposes a boundless heroism to vanquish either by harassing or by annihilating the enemy according to circumstances, and by combining military operations with political and economic action; no fixed line of demarcation, the front being wherever the enemy is found.

Concentration of troops to realize an overwhelming superiority over the enemy where he is sufficiently exposed in order to destroy his manpower; initiative, suppleness, rapidity, surprise, suddenness in attack and retreat. As long as the strategic balance of forces remains disadvantageous, resolutely to muster troops to obtain absolute superiority in combat in a given place, and at a given time. To exhaust little by little by small victories the enemy forces and at the same time to maintain and increase ours. In these concrete conditions it proves absolutely necessary not to lose sight of the main objective of the fighting that is the destruction of the enemy manpower. Therefore losses must be avoided even at the cost of losing ground. And that for the purpose of recovering, later on, the occupied territories and completely liberating the country.

In the war of liberation in Viet Nam, guerilla activities spread to all the regions temporarily occupied by the enemy. Each inhabitant was a soldier, each village a fortress, each Party cell, each village administrative committee a staff.

The people as a whole took part in the armed struggle, fighting according to the principles of guerilla warfare, in small packets, but always in pursuance of the one and same line, and the same instructions, those of the Central Committee of the Party and the Government.

At variance with numerous other countries which waged revolutionary wars, Viet Nam, in the first years of its struggle, did not and could not engage in pitched battles. It had to rest content with guerilla warfare. At the cost of thousands of difficulties and countless sacrifices, this guerilla war developed progressively into a form of mobile war that daily increased in scale. While retaining certain characteristics of guerilla war, it involved regular campaigns with greater attacks on fortified positions. Starting from small operations with the strength of a platoon or a company to annihilate a few men or a group of enemy soldiers, our army went over, later, to more important combats with a battalion or regiment to cut one or several enemy companies to pieces, finally coming to greater campaigns bringing into play many regiments, then many divisions to end at Dien Bien Phu where the French Expeditionary Corps lost 16,000 men of its crack units. It was this process of development that enabled our army to move forward steadily on the road to victory.

People's war, long term war, guerilla warfare developing step by-step into mobile warfare, such are the most valuable lessons of the war of liberation in Viet Nam. It was by following that line that the Party led the Resistance to victory. After three thousand days of fighting, difficulties and sacrifices, our people defeated the French imperialists and American interventionists. At present, in the liberated half of our country, sixteen million of our compatriots, by their creative labour, are healing the horrible wounds of war, reconstructing the country and building socialism. In the meantime the struggle is going on to achieve the democratic national revolution throughout the country and to reunify the Fatherland on the basis of independence and democracy.

II

After this account of the main lines of the war of liberation waged by the Vietnamese people against the French and American imperialists, I shall speak of the Viet Nam People's Army.

Being the armed forces of the Vietnamese people, it was born and grew up in the flames of the war of national liberation. Its embryo was the self-defence units created by the Nghe An Soviets which managed to hold power for a few months in the period of revolutionary upsurge in the years 1930-1931. But the creation of revolutionary armed forces was positively considered only at the outset of World War Two when the preparation for an armed insurrection came to the fore of our attention. Our military and paramilitary formations appeared at the Bac Son uprising and in the revolutionary bases in Cao Bang region. Following the setting up of the first platoon of National Salvation, on December 22, 1944, another platoon-strong unit was created : the Progaganda unit of the Viet Nam Liberation Army. Our war bases organised during illegality were at the time limited to a few districts in the provinces of Cao Bang, Bac Can and Lang Son in the jungle of the North. As for the revolutionary armed forces they still consisted of people's units of self-defence and a few groups and platoons completely free from production work. Their number increased quickly and there were already several thousands of guerillas at the beginning of 1945, at the coup de force by the Japanese fascists over the French colonialists. At the time of the setting up of the people's power in the rural regions of six provinces in Viet Bac which were established as a free zone, the existing armed organisations merged to form the Viet Nam Liberation Army.

During the August insurrection, side by side with the people and the self-defence units, the Liberation Army took part in the conquest of power. By incorporating the paramilitary forces regrouped in the course of the glorious days of August, it saw its strength increase rapidly. With a heterogeneous material wrested from the Japanese and their Bao An troops — rifles alone consisted of sixteen different types including old French patterns and even rifles of the czarist forces taken by the Japanese — this young and poorly equipped army soon had to face the aggression of the French Expeditionary Corps which had modern armaments. Such antiquated equipment required from the Vietnamese army and people complete self-sacrifice and superhuman heroism.

Should the enemy attack the regions where our troops were stationed, the latter would give battle. Should he ferret about in the large zones where there were no regular formations, the people would stay his advance with rudimentary weapons : sticks, spears, scimitars, bows, flintlocks. From the first days, there appeared three types of armed forces : para-military organisations or guerilla units, regional troops and regular units. These formations were, in the field of organisation, the expression of the general mobilisation of the people in arms. They co-operated closely with one another to annihilate the enemy.

Peasants, workers and intellectuals crowded into the ranks of the armed forces of the Revolution. Leading cadres of the Party and the State apparatus became officers from the first moment. The greatest difficulty to be solved was the equipment problem. Throughout Viet Nam there was no factory manufacturing war materials. Throughout nearly a century, possession and use of arms were strictly forbidden by the colonial administration. Importation was impossible, the neighbouring countries being hostile to the Democratic Republic of Viet Nam. The sole source of supply could only be the battlefront: to take the material from the enemy to turn it against him. While carrying on the aggression against Viet Nam the French Expeditionary Corps fulfilled another task: it became, unwittingly, the supplier of the Viet Nam People's Army with French, even U.S. arms. In spite of their enormous efforts, the arms factories set up later on with makeshift means were far from being able to meet all our needs. A great part of our military materials came from war-booty.

As I have stressed, the Viet Nam People's Army could at first bring into combat only small units such as platoons or companies. The regular forces were, at a given time, compelled to split up into companies operating separately to promote the extension of guerilla activities while mobile battalions were maintained for more important actions. After each victorious combat, the people's armed forces marked a new step forward.

Tempered in combat and stimulated by victories, the guerilla formations created conditions for the growth of the regional troops. And the latter, in their turn, promoted the development of the regular forces. For nine successive years, by following this heroic path bristling with difficulties, our people's army grew up with a determination to win at all costs. It became an army of hundreds of thousands strong, successively amalgamating into regiments and divisions and directing towards a progressive standardisation in organisation and equipment. This force, ever more politically conscious, and better trained militarily, succeeded in fighting and defeating the five hundred thousand men of the French Expeditionary Corps who were equipped and supplied by the United States.

* * *

The Vietnamese Army is indeed a *national one.* In fighting against imperialism and the traitors in its service, it has fought for national independence and the unity of the country. In its ranks are the finest sons of Viet Nam, the most sincere patriots from all revolutionary classes, from all nationalities — majority as well as minority people. It symbolises the irresistible rousing of the national conscience, the union of the entire Vietnamese people in the fight against imperialist aggression to save the country.

Our army is a *democratic army,* because it fights for the people's democratic interests, and the defence of people's democratic power. Impregnated with the principles of democracy in its internal political life, it submits to a rigorous discipline, but one freely consented to.

Our army is a *people's army,* because it defends the fundamental interests of the people, in the first place those of the toiling people, workers and peasants. As regards social composition, it comprises a great majority of picked fighters of peasant and worker origin, and intellectuals faithful to the cause of the Revolution.

It is *the true army of the people, of toilers, the army of workers and peasants, led by the Party of the working class.* Throughout the war of national liberation, its aims of struggle were the very ones followed by the Party and people : independence of the nation, and land to the tillers. Since the return of peace, as a tool of proletarian dictatorship, its mission is to defend the socialist revolution and socialist building in the North, to support the political struggle for the peaceful reunification of the country, and to contribute to the strengthening of peace in Indo-China and South-east Asia.

In the first of the ten points of his Oath of Honour, the fighter of the Viet Nam People's Army swears :

" To sacrifice himself unreservedly for the Fatherland, fight for the cause of national independence, democracy and socialism, under the leadership of the Viet Nam Workers' Party and of the Government of the Democratic Republic, to build a peaceful, reunified, independent, democratic and prosperous Viet Nam and contribute to the strengthening of peace in South-east Asia and the world. "

This is precisely what makes the Viet Nam People's Army a true child of the people. The people, in return, give it unsparing affection and support. Therein lies the inexhaustible source of its power.

The Viet Nam People's Army has been created by the Party, which ceaselessly trains and educates it. It has always been and will always be under the *leadership of the Party* which, alone, has made it into a revolutionary army, a true people's army. Since its creation and in the course of its development, this leadership by the Party has been made concrete on the organisational plan. The army has

54

always had its political commissars. In the units, the military and political chiefs assume their responsibilities under the leadership of the Party Committee at the corresponding echelon.

The People's Army is the instrument of the Party and of the revolutionary State for the accomplishment, in armed form, of the tasks of the revolution. Profound awareness of the aims of the Party, boundless loyalty to the cause of the nation and the working class, and a spirit of unreserved sacrifice are fundamental questions for the army, and questions of principle. Therefore, the political work in its ranks is of the first importance. *It is the soul of the army.* In instilling Marxist-Leninist ideology into the army, it aims at raising the army's political consciousness and ideological level, at strengthening the class position of its cadres and soldiers. During the liberation war, this work imbued the army with the policy of long-drawn-out resistance and the imperative necessity for the people and army to rely on their own strength to overcome difficulties. It instilled into the army the profound significance of mass mobilisation in order to achieve rent reduction and agrarian reform, which had a decisive effect on the morale of the troops. In the new stage entered upon since the restoration of peace, political work centres on the line of socialist revolution in the North and of struggle for the reunification of the country.

But that is not all. Political work still bears upon the correct fulfilment in the army of the programmes of the Party and Government, and the setting up of good relations with the population and between officers and men. It aims at maintaining and strengthening combativeness, uniting true patriotism with proletarian internationalism, developing revolutionary heroism and the great tradition of our army summed up in its slogan : " Resolved to fight, determined to win ". Political work is the work of propaganda among and education of the masses ; it is, furthermore, the organisational work of the Party in the army. We have always given particular attention to the strengthening of organisations of the Party in the units. From 35 to 40 per cent of officers and armymen have joined it, among the officers, the percentage even exceeds 90 per cent.

The Viet Nam People's Army has always seen to establishing and maintaining *good relations with the people.* These are based upon the identity of their aims of struggle : in fact, the people and army are together in the fight against the enemy to save the Fatherland, and ensure the full success of the task of liberating the nation and the working class. The people are to the army what water is to fish, as the saying goes. And this saying has a profound significance. Our Army fought on the front ; is has also worked to educate the people and helped them to the best of its ability. The Vietnamese fighter has always taken care to observe point 9 of its Oath of Honour :

" In contacts with the people, to follow these three recommendations :

— To respect the people

— To help the people

— To defend the people... in order to win their confidence and affection and achieve a perfect understanding between the people and the army ".

Our army has always organised days of help for peasants in production work and in the struggle against flood and drought. It has always observed a correct attitude in its relations with the people. It has never done injury to their property, not even a needle or a bit of thread. During the Resistance, especially in the enemy rear, it brought everything into play to defend ordinary people's lives and property ; in the newly liberated regions, it strictly carried out the orders of the Party and Government, which enabled it to win the unreserved support of the broadest masses, even in the minority peoples' regions and catholic villages. Since the return of peace, thousands of its officers and men have participated in the great movements for the accomplishment of agrarian reform for agricultural collectivisation and socialist transformation of handicrafts, industry and private trade. It has actively taken part in the economic recovery, and in socialist work days. It has participated in the building of lines of communication, it has built its own barracks and cleared land to found State farms.

The Viet Nam People's Army is always concerned to establish and maintain *good relations between officers and men as well as between the officers themselves.* Originating from the working strata, officers and men also serve the people's interests and unstintingly devote themselves to the cause of the nation and the working class. Of course every one of them has particular responsibilities which devolve upon him. But relations of comradeship based on political equality and fraternity of class have been established between them. The officer likes his men ; he must not only guide them in their work and studies, but take an interest in their life and take into consideration their desires and initiatives. As for the soldier, he must respect his superiors and correctly fulfil all their orders. The officer of the People's Army must set a good example from all points of view : to show himself to be resolute, brave, to ensure discipline and internal democracy, to know how to achieve perfect unity among his men. He must behave like a chief, a leader, vis-à-vis the masses in his unit. The basis of these relations between army-men and officers, like those between officers or between soldiers is solidarity in the fight, and mutual affection of brothers-in-arms, love at the same time pure and sublime, tested and forged in the battle, in the struggle for the defence of the Fatherland and the people.

The Viet Nam People's Army practises a strict *discipline*, allied to a wide internal *democracy*. As requires point 2 of its Oath of Honour : " The fighter must rigorously carry out the orders of his superiors and throw himself body and soul into the immediate and strict fulfilment of the tasks entrusted to him ". Can we say that guerilla warfare did not require severe discipline ? Of course not. It is true that it asked the commander and leader to allow each unit or each region a certain margin of initiative in order to undertake every positive action that it might think opportune. But a centralised leadership and a unified command at a given degree always proved to be necessary. He who speaks of the army, speaks of strict discipline.

Such a discipline is not in contradiction with the internal democracy of our troops. In cells, executive committees of the Party at various levels as well as in plenary meetings of fighting units, the application of principles of democratic centralism is the rule. The facts have proved that the more democracy is respected within the units, the more unity will be strengthened, discipline raised, and orders carried out. The combativeness of the army will thereby be all the greater.

The restoration of peace has created in Viet Nam a new situation. The North is entirely liberated, but the South is still under the yoke of American imperialists and the

Ngo Dinh Diem clique, their lackeys. North Viet Nam has entered the stage of socialist revolution while the struggle is going on to free the South from colonial and feudal fetters. To safeguard peace and socialist construction, to help in making the North a strong rampart for the peaceful reunification of the country, the problem of forces of national defence should not be neglected. The People's Army must face the bellicose aims of American imperialists and their lackeys and step by step become *a regular and modern army.*

First of all, it is important to stress that, in the process of its transformation into a regular and modern army, our army always remains a revolutionary army, a people's army. That is the fundamental characteristic that makes the people's regular and modern army in the North differ radically from Ngo Dinh Diem's army, a regular and modern army too, but anti-revolutionary, anti-popular and in the hands of the people's enemies. The People's Army must necessarily see to the strengthening of the leadership of Party and political work. It must work further to consolidate the solidarity between officers and men, between the troops and the people, raise the spirit of self-conscious discipline, while maintaining internal democracy. Taking steps to that end, the Party has during the last years, given a prominent place to the activities of its organisations as well as to the political work in the army. Officers, warrant officers and armymen, all of them have followed political courses to improve their understanding of the tasks of socialist revolution and the struggle for national reunification, consolidating their class standpoint and strengthening Marxist-Leninist ideology. This is a particularly important question, more especially as the People's Army has grown up in an agricultural country, and has in its ranks a great majority of toiling peasants and urban petty-bourgeois. Our fighters have gone through a dogged political education and their morale has been forged in the combat. However, the struggle against the influence of bourgeois and petty-bourgeois ideology remains necessary. Thanks to the strengthening of ideological work, the army has become an efficacious instrument in the service of proletarian dictatorship, and has been entirely faithful to the cause of socialist revolution and national reunification. The new advances realised by it in the political plan have found their full expression in the movement "with giant strides, let us overfulfil the norms of the programme," a broad mass movement which is developing among our troops, parallel with the socialist emulation movement among the working people in North Viet Nam.

It is essential actively and firmly to continue, on the basis of a constant strengthening of political consciousness, the progressive transformation of the People's Army into a regular and modern army. Thanks to the development realised during the last years of the Resistance War, our army, which was made up of infantry-men only, is now *an army composed of different arms.* If the problem of improvement of equipments and technique is important, that of cadres and soldiers capable of using them is more important. Our army has always been concerned with the training of officers and warrant officers of worker and peasant origin or revolutionary intellectuals tested under fire. It helps them raise their cultural and technical level to become competent officers and warrant officers of a regular and modern army.

To raise the fighting power of the army, to bring about a strong centralisation of command and a close cooperation between the different arms, it is indispensable to enforce *regulations fitted to a regular army.* It is not that nothing has been done in this field during the years of the Resistance War; it is a matter of perfecting the existing regulations. The main thing is not to lose sight of the principle that any new regulation must draw its inspiration from the popular character of the army and the absolute necessity of maintaining the leadership of the Party. Along with the general regulations, the statute of officers has been promulgated ; a correct system of wages has taken the place of the former regime of allowances in kind ; the question of rewards and decorations has been regularised. All these measures have resulted in the strengthening of discipline and solidarity within the army, and of the sense of responsibility among officers and warrant officers as well as among soldiers.

Military training, and political education, are key tasks in the building of the army in peace-time. The question of fighting regulations, and that of tactical concepts and appropriate tactical principles gain a particular importance. The question is to synthesize past experiences, and analyse well the concrete conditions of our army in organization and equipment, consider our economic structure, the terrain of the country — land of forests and jungles, of plains and fields. The question is to assimilate well the modern military science of the armies of the brother countries. Unceasing efforts are indispensable in the training of troops and the development of cadres.

For many years, the Viet Nam People's Army was based on voluntary service : all officers and soldiers voluntarily enlisted for an undetermined period. Its ranks swelled by the affluence of youth always ready to answer the appeal of the Fatherland. Since the return of peace, it has become necessary to replace voluntary service by *compulsory military service*. This substitution has met with warm response from the population. A great number of volunteers, after demobilisation returned to fields and factories; others are working in units assigned to production work, thus making an active contribution to the building of socialism. Conscription is enforced on the basis of the strengthening and development of the self-defence organisations in the communes, factories and schools. The members of these para-military organisations are ready not only to rejoin the permanent army, of which they constitute a particularly important reserve, but also to ensure the security and defence of their localities.

The People's Army was closely linked with the national liberation war, in the fire of which it was born and grew up. At present, its development should neither be disassociated from the building of socialism in the North, nor from the people's struggle for a reunified independent and democratic Viet Nam. Confident of the people's affection and support, in these days of peace as during the war, the People's Army will achieve its tasks: to defend peace and the Fatherland.

III

"...As is said above, the history of the national liberation war of the Vietnamese people, that of the Viet Nam People's Army, is the history of the victory of a weak nation, of a colonised people who rose up against the aggressive forces of an imperialist power. This victory is also that of Marxism-Leninism applied to the armed revolutionary struggle in a colonised country, that of the Party of the working class in the leadership of the revolution that it heads, in the democratic national stage as well as in the socialist one.

The vanguard Party of the Vietnamese working people, headed by President Ho Chi Minh, the great leader of the people and the nation, is the organiser and guide that has led the Vietnamese people and their army to victory. In the light of Marxism-Leninism applied to the national democratic revolution in a colonised country, it has made a sound analysis of the contradictions of that society, and stated clearly the fundamental tasks of the revolution. On the question of the national liberation war, it has dialectically analysed the balance of opposing forces and mapped out appropriate strategy and tactics. In the light of Marxism-Leninism, it has created and led a heroic people's army. It has ceaselessly instilled revolutionary spirit and the true patriotism of the proletariat into the people and their army.

The Party has known how to learn from the valuable experiences of the October Revolution which, with the Soviet Red Army, showed the road of liberation not only to the workers of the capitalist countries, but also to colonial people ; and those of the Chinese Revolution and Liberation Army which have enriched the theories of the national democratic revolution, of revolutionary war and army in a semi-colonised country. Their wonderful examples have ceaselessly lighted the road of the struggle and successes of the Vietnamese people. In combining the invaluable experiences of the Soviet Union and People's China with its own, our Party has always taken into account the concrete reality of the revolutionary war in Viet Nam, thus is able in its turn to enrich the theories of revolutionary war and army.

At present, on the international plane, the forces of socialist countries, led by the Soviet Union, have become a power previously unknown ; the national liberation movement has developed considerably everywhere ; the possibilities for achieving lasting peace in the world are greater. However, imperialism is still pursuing its war preparations and seeking to strengthen its military alliance for aggression. While there is a certain relaxation of tension in the international situation, South-east Asia still remains one of the centres of tension in the world. American imperialism is ceaselessly strengthening its military and political hold on the South of our country. It is pursuing the same policy of interference in Laos, aimed at turning it into a colony and military base for a new war of aggression.

Profoundly peace-loving, the Vietnamese people and their army support every effort for disarmament, every effort to relax tension and establish a lasting peace. But they must at the same time heighten their vigilance, strengthen their combativeness, increase their potentiality for defence, and contribute to strengthening the fraternal bonds between the peoples and the revolutionary armed forces of the socialist countries. They are determined to fulfil their sacred duties : to defend the work of socialist revolution and the building of socialism in the North, to pursue the struggle for the peaceful reunification of the Fatherland, to be ready to break every imperialist attempt to provoke a war of aggression, and to contribute to the safeguarding of peace in South-east Asia and throughout the world.

THE GREAT EXPERIENCES GAINED
BY OUR PARTY IN LEADING THE
ARMED STRUGGLE AND BUILDING
REVOLUTIONARY
ARMED FORCES

Our Party was born at a time when the revolutionary movement was growing in our country. From the first days, the Party led the peasants to carry out armed uprising and establish Soviet power. Therefore, the Party soon gained a knowledge of the problems of revolutionary power and armed struggle. As Marxism-Leninism teaches, the question of State power is the most important question in every revolution, and the way of setting up revolutionary power, " the only way of liberation " is " the way of armed struggle of the masses ". [1]

The 1930-1931 movement was put down ; our Party continued to lead the masses to carry on political struggle, sometimes illegally, sometimes semi-legally, endeavouring to restore the revolutionary bases to push the movement forward. In 1939, when World War Two broke out, the situation in the world and at home underwent changes, and the question of preparation for armed uprising aimed at liberating the nation again arose. From that time, our Party led our people to prepare for armed uprising and successfully carry out the general insurrection in August 1945 ; then for 9 years on end, our Party led the long Resistance War of our people to victory.

During the first 15 years of the 30 years of revolutionary mobilisation, the Party was in an illegal position ; afterwards, revolutionary power was founded all over the

---

[1] The Program of Action of the Indochinese Communist Party, 1932

country and the Party became a Party in power. Since the State has been under the leadership of the Party, in the years of armed struggle as well as in recent years after the restoration of peace, the building of the revolutionary armed forces has always been regarded as one of the most important tasks of the Party, because the revolutionary armed forces are the main part of the revolutionary State.

Looking back over the path covered, it is obvious that the armed struggle has played a very important part in the process of the revolutionary mobilisation of our people under the leadership of the Party. Through the years of extremely hard and valiant armed struggle, our Party accumulated most valuable experiences. The study of these experiences is of great significance for the strengthening of the revolutionary armed forces, for the consolidation of national defence in the North, as well as for the completion of the national democratic revolution throughout the country.

Revolutionary armed struggle in any country has common fundamental laws. Revolutionary armed struggle in each country has characteristics and laws of its own too.

Russia was originally an imperialist country, with capitalist economy developed to a certain extent. The Russian October Revolution was an uprising of the working class and the urban labouring people to overthrow capitalism, and to establish the worker-peasant Soviet power. The revolutionary war that followed it was the revolutionary civil war of the Soviet labouring people against the white guards of the reactionary bourgeoisie and landlord class ; at the same time, it was the war to defend the socialist Fatherland against the interventionist joint armies of fourteen capitalist countries. Later, the great war for the defence of the Soviet Union against the aggressive fascist armies was a revolutionary war of the labouring people of a socialist country which had become powerful, but was still encircled by capitalism.

China was a semi-colonial and semi-feudal country, covering an immense area, with the biggest population in the world and a backward agricultural economy. For a long period, the armed struggle in China was the long-term revolutionary civil war waged by the Chinese people against the feudal forces and the bureaucratic capitalists, henchmen of the imperialists. In the resistance war, this was a long-term war of the Chinese people against the aggressive imperialists. This armed struggle aimed at achieving the political goals of the national democratic revolution and paving the way for the Chinese revolution to advance to socialism.

Viet Nam was a small, weak, colonial and semi-feudal country, covering a fairly small area, with a small population and an extremely backward agricultural economy. There was the struggle of the people throughout the country, under forms of armed uprising and long-term resistance to overthrow imperialism and the reactionary feudal forces. The aim was to realise the political goals of the national democratic revolution as in China, to recover national independence and bring land to the peasants, creating conditions for the advance of the revolution of our country to socialism.

Therefore, the revolutionary armed struggle in Viet Nam was naturally the reflection of the laws of the revolutionary armed struggle in general, but simultaneously it had its own characteristics and laws. The success of our Party in leading the revolutionary armed struggle and in building revolutionary armed forces is the success of Marxism-Leninism. This is the success of wise and creative application of Marxist-Leninist principles on revolutionary war and revolutionary armed forces to the practical situation of a small, weak, colonial and semi-feudal country which had to fight for a long period against a powerful enemy while encircled by imperialism.

OUR PARTY SUCCESSFULLY LED THE PREPARATION FOR THE ARMED UPRISING AND THE AUGUST 1945 GENERAL INSURRECTION

In 1939, immediately after the outbreak of World War Two in Europe, the Party Central Committee realised in time that a new cycle of war and revolution had begun, " the situation in Indo-China has advanced to the stage of national liberation ". In 1940 and early 1941, insurrections broke out successively in Bac Son, Nam Ky and Do Luong. Although these uprisings were ferociously repressed by the enemy, they were, however, " the signs of the national insurrection and the first steps of armed struggle of the Indochinese peoples. " (1)

In fact, in the very difficult conditions prevailing at that time, our people lived very miserably under the double yoke of the French and Japanese imperialists, and the revolutionary movement was mercilessly repressed. But our Party continued to do its utmost to step up propaganda and agitation among the people, to gather all patriotic forces into the Viet Minh, to build guerilla bases, set up revolutionary armed forces and make preparations for armed insurrection.

(1) Resolution of the 8th Session of the Central Committee. 1941.

In August 1945, the armies of the Soviet Union and the Allied powers were completely victorious. The Japanese fascists surrendered. An atmosphere of insurrection was seething all over Viet Nam. Millions of people in the towns and countryside demonstrated and displayed their forces. The general insurrection broke out. The August Revolution was victorious. On September 2nd, President Ho Chi Minh, on behalf of the provisional government, read the Declaration of Independence before the Vietnamese people and the world. The Democratic Republic of Viet Nam came into being, the first people's democratic country in Southeast Asia.

The August General Insurrection ended in a great victory : the high tide of the struggle against the French and Japanese fascists waged by the Vietnamese people during World War Two overthrew the near century-old imperialist domination and the thousand-years-old monarchy, to set up the democratic republican regime. The August General Insurrection opened a new era in the history of the Vietnamese people, an era in which they took their destiny into their own hands.

The preparations for the insurrection during World War Two, and the August insurrection taught us many valuable lessons. In his book, *The August Revolution*, comrade Truong Chinh has analysed the strong and the weak points of this revolution and made many apt observations. In this article, we shall deal with the whole process of the preparation for armed insurrection to the victory of the general insurrection, pointing out some of the main experiences which are also a great success for the leadership of our Party.

1. The August general insurrection was successful, first of all, because of the correct strategic guidance of the Party Central Committee in the question of national liberation. The Central Committee regarded it as the main task for the whole Party and for the entire people and deemed it necessary to rally all patriotic forces in order to carry it out successfully and by every means

Our country was a colonial and semi-feudal one. The two basic contradictions in our society were the contradiction between imperialism and our nation and the contradiction between the feudal landlord class and our people, chiefly the peasantry ; of these two contradictions, that between imperialism and our nation had to be considered as the most essential. That is why the revolution in Viet Nam, which was a national democratic revolution, had two fundamental tasks : the anti-imperialist and the anti-feudal task. Among these two tasks, the anti-imperialists task, the task of wiping out imperialism to liberate the people, had to be regarded as the most essential. After 1930, the Party analysed the two contradictions in our society and laid down the two tasks of our revolution, thereby mobilising a wide and deep revolutionary movement. But it was not until 1939-1941 that the anti-imperialist task, the task of national liberation was clearly conceived as the most essential. Moreover, due to the appreciation of the great events in the world and at home at that time, the Party set the national liberation task as an urgent one for the whole people.

The 6th session of the Central Committee held late in 1939, clearly pointed out : " Nowadays, the situation has changed. At the present time, French imperialism has taken part in launching a world war. The domination imposed on colonies such as Indo-China, which is clearly a fascist militarist regime, and the scheme of compromising and surrendering to Japan have set a vital problem before the Indochinese people. *In the life and death struggle of the Indochinese nations there is no way out other than that of overthrowing French imperialism, opposing all foreign invaders, either white or yellow-skinned, in order to regain liberation and independence.*"

The 8th enlarged session of the Central Committee held in 1941 perfected the change of direction in the Party's leadership of the Revolution and mapped out the concrete political program for the national liberation revolution. It was estimated by the Session that "at the present time, the watchword of the Party is first *to liberate the Indochinese people from the Japanese and French yoke.* For the fulfilment of these tasks, the forces of the whole of Indo-China must be concentrated, those who love their country will unite together into a Front and rally all their forces to fight for national independence and freedom, to smash the French and the Japanese invaders. The alliance of all forces of the classes and parties, the patriotic revolutionary groups, religious groups and all people fighting the Japanese, is the essential work of our Party."

The Central Committee also put out a *New policy for the Party*, temporarily put aside its slogan for agrarian reform and replaced it by the slogan of reduction of land rents and interest charges, and confiscation of land belonging to imperialists and Vietnamese traitors and its distribution to the peasants. Simultaneously, it decided to found the League for Independence of Viet Nam (called

Viet Minh for short) and various organisations for national salvation.

Stressing the task of national liberation, the resolution of the 8th session of the Central Committee was extremely precise and clear, and conformed to the conditions prevailing at that time, to the deep and fundamental aspirations of each class and each patriotic stratum. It was precisely for this reason that within a short period, the Viet Minh gathered together the great forces of the people and became the most powerful political organisation of the broad revolutionary masses. The program of the Viet Minh was warmly welcomed by all sections of the people. The Viet Minh was well known throughout the country. The resolution of the 8th session of the Central Committee was a concrete platform which had a decisive effect on the victory of the August Revolution.

It is necessary to add that at that time, from the strategic point of view, the feudal landlord class was not definitely assessed as the object of the revolution. From the theoretical point of view, national liberation was somewhat seen as being apart from the bourgeois democratic revolution; as far as the immediate task was concerned, the landlord class was too highly evaluated and there was lack of consideration for the worker-peasant alliance in the National United Front. These shortcomings were to have an influence on the thinking and work of our Party in the future; for instance, they led partly to the slighting of the anti-feudal task in the first years of seizure of power and of the Resistance War.

2. The August general insurrection triumphed because, while pointing out the above-mentioned change of direction for the revolutionary task, the Party Central Committee timely laid down the change of the forms of struggle and put forward the question of preparing for armed insurrection

The shifting from political struggle to armed struggle was a very great change that required a long period of preparation. If insurrection is said to be an art, the main content of this art is to know how to give to the struggle forms appropriate to the political situation at each stage, how to maintain the correct relation between the forms of political struggle and those of armed struggle in each period. At the beginning, the political struggle was the main task, the armed struggle a secondary one. Gradually, both the political struggle and armed struggle became equally important. Later, we went forward to the stage when the armed struggle occupied the key role. But even in this period, we had to define clearly when it occupied the key role within only a certain region and when throughout the nation. We had to base ourselves on the guiding principle with regard to forms of struggle to clearly lay down the guiding principles for our work and for the forms of organisation. In the then situation, the struggle between the enemy and us was extremely hard and fierce. If guidance in struggle and organisation was not precise, that is to say did not correctly follow the guiding principle of both determination and carefulness, and of knowing how to estimate the subjective conditions and compare the revolutionary forces with the counter-revolutionary forces, we would certainly have met with difficulty and failure. The correct leadership in the preparation for armed insurrection had to secure steady and timely development of the revolutionary forces until the time for launching the insurrection was ripe.

It was clearly pointed out at the 8th session of the Central Committee: "To prepare forces for an insurrection, our Party has to:

"1 — Develop and consolidate the organisations for national salvation.

"2 — Expand the organisations to the cities, enterprises, mines and plantations.

"3 — Expand the organisations to the provinces where the revolutionary movement is still weak and to the minority areas.

"4 — Steel the Party members' spirit of determination and sacrifice.

"5 — Steel the Party members so that they may have capacity and experience to enable them to lead and cope with the situation.

"6 — Form small guerilla groups and soldiers' organisations..."

When speaking of insurrection, V. Lenin stressed that "uprising must rely upon the high tide of the revolutionary movement of the masses", and "not upon a conspiracy". To speak of preparations for armed insurrection and of insurrection does not mean that we will pay no more attention to the political movement of the masses; on the contrary, insurrection could not be victorious without a deep and wide political movement waged by the revolutionary masses. Therefore, to make good preparations for armed insurrection, the most essential and important task was to make propaganda among the masses and organise them, to "develop and consolidate the organisations for national salvation ". Only on the basis of strong political organisations could semi-armed organisations be set up firmly, guerilla groups and guerilla units organised which have close connection with the revolutionary masses, eventually to further their activities and development.

In the early years, as the political movement of the masses was not strong enough and the enemy's forces still stable, the political mobilisation among the masses had all the more to be considered as the main task for the preparation of armed insurrection. The propaganda and organisation of the masses carried out everywhere in the country, particularly at the key points was of decisive importance. Viet Bac mountain regions were soon chosen by the Party Central Committee as the armed bases, the two central areas being Bac Son - Vu Nhai and Cao Bang. In the then conditions, the armed bases must be held secret, must be localities where the revolutionary movement was firm and the mass organisations strong; on the basis of the political organisations of the masses, self-defence groups and fighting self-defence groups (1) were set up which swelled afterwards to local armed groups, or armed platoons freed or partially freed from production, and eventually to bigger guerilla units. Underground operating cadres' teams, underground militarized teams, armed shock teams and local armed groups and platoons gradually appeared. The most

---

(1) Self-defence force ensures public security and order in the village and take part in the fighting in the last extremity only. Fighting self-defence force has the task to fight the enemy as soon as he arrives at the village.

appropriate guiding principle for activities was *armed propaganda (1); political activities were more important than military activities, and fighting less important than propaganda ;* armed activity was used to safeguard, consolidate and develop the political bases. Once the political bases were consolidated and developed, we proceeded one step further to the consolidation and development of the semi-armed and armed forces. These had to be in strict secrecy with central points for propaganda activity or for dealing with traitors. Their military attacks were strictly secret and carried out with rapidity. Their movements had to be phantom-like. A position of legal struggle was maintained for the broad masses. The setting up of revolutionary power was not then opportune. There were regions in which the whole masses took part in organisations of national salvation, and the village Viet Minh Committees had, as a matter of course, full prestige among the masses as an underground organisation of the revolutionary power. But even in these localities, we had not to attempt to overthrow the enemy, but try to win over and make use of him. It was in keeping with that direction that the Party Central Committee gave instructions to the armed units for national salvation at Bac Son-Vu Nhai. It was in line with that direction that President Ho Chi Minh pointed out the guiding principle of armed propaganda for the armed organisations at Cao Bang - Bac Can, chiefly when giving orders for the setting up of the Viet Nam Liberation Armed Propaganda Unit. Experiences have proved that in the first period of the preparation for armed insurrection, if the above-mentioned guiding principles were not thoroughly understood, the revolutionary movement would

---

(1) Propaganda carried out by armed units.

often meet with temporary difficulties and losses, thus affecting the preparation for armed insurrection.

With the Japanese Coup de force on March 9, 1945, the situation underwent great changes. The French fascists collapsed. Japanese fascism, the main immediate enemy of the Vietnamese people, had not yet time to consolidate its rule in Indo-China and was suffering successive defeats on various battlefields. The Party Central Committee realised very clearly and timely the new political crisis caused by the Japanese Coup d'Etat and issued the order "to mobilise a strong high tide of anti-Japanese movement for national salvation which would be the prerequisite for the general insurrection". Preparations were made to be ready to shift to the general uprising when conditions were ripe. The Party Central Committee also worked out the policy of "promoting guerilla warfare to occupy the resistance bases", brought all armed forces under a single command and set up revolutionary power in areas where the guerillas were operating. Where mass bases were fairly strong, power was exercised secretly.

From Cao Bang - Bac Can to Thai Nguyen - Tuyen Quang and in several localities in the Midland, the Liberation Armed Propaganda units and National Salvation units attacked the district towns and set up revolutionary power. The attacks on Japanese paddy stores developed strongly everywhere, the picked-units of the Viet Minh operated right in the cities. The network of self-defence and fighting self-defence units, People's committees and Liberation Committees spread to all localities. In Quang Ngai province, the Ba To guerilla unit was born. A seething atmosphere prevailed in the whole country.

In April 1945, the Military Conference of north Viet Nam decided to unify the revolutionary armed forces under the name of Viet Nam Liberation Army ; resistance zones were set up, and the North Viet Nam Revolutionary Military Committee organised. In June, the free zone was founded, the ten-point policy of the Viet Minh being implemented everywhere in the 6 provinces of the free zone. The Viet Minh was gaining increasing strength. The influence of the free zone and that of the Liberation Army which spread widely and rapidly, further encouraged our people to prepare to take advantage of the good opportunity, winning the wavering elements to side with the revolutionary forces, and throwing the enemy's ranks into confusion.

After May 1945, the preparation for armed insurrection entered a new stage with the following features : *the upsurge of the anti-Japanese movement for national salvation strongly increased everywhere, regional guerilla war was launched ; local revolutionary power was established, and anti-Japanese bases set up.* Under the leadership of our Party, the movement advanced boldly and firmly.

3. The August General Insurrection was successful because the Party Central Committee accurately and clearsightedly laid down what the conditions should be for the General Insurrection to break out and gain success ; this therefore, would help mobilise the whole Party and the entire people, promote the spirit of determination, courage, positiveness and creativeness of the masses.

When speaking of insurrection, J. Stalin pointed out that selecting the right opportunity is one of the essential conditions to lead the uprising to victory : " The selection of the moment for the decisive blow, of the moment for starting the insurrection, so timed as to coincide with the moment when the crisis has reached its climax, when it is already the case that the vanguard is prepared to fight to the end, the reserves are prepared to support the vanguard, and maximum consternation reigns in the ranks of the enemy "

Our Party had drawn bloody experiences from the Nghe - Tinh and Nam Ky insurrections. All these spoke out the decisive importance of the right opportunity for uprising. Therefore, as early as 1941, the 8th session of the Central Committee took care to clearly set out what the conditions should be when people could be led to carry out the insurrection : " The revolution in Indo-China must be ended with an armed uprising ; in order to wage an armed insurrection, conditions must be as follows :

" the National Salvation Front is already unified all over the country ;

" the masses can no longer live under the French-Japanese yoke, and are ready to sacrifice themselves in launching the insurrection ;

" the ruling circles in Indo-China are driven to an economic, political and military crisis ;

" the objective conditions are favourable to the uprising such as the Chinese army's great triumph over the Japanese army, the outbreak of the French or Japanese revolution, the total victory of the democratic camp in the Pacific and in the Soviet Union, the revolutionary fermentation in the French and Japanese colonies, and particularly the landing of Chinese or British-American armies in Indo-China "

The instruction on the *preparations for the Insurrection* issued by the Viet Minh Central Committee in May, 1944, also pointed out clearly the moment the people should rise up :

" 1. The enemy's ranks at that moment are divided and dismayed to the extreme.

" 2. The organisations for national salvation and the revolutionaries are resolved to rise up and kill the enemy.

" 3. Broad masses wholeheartedly support the uprising and determinedly help the vanguard.

" If we launch the insurrection at the right time, our revolution for national liberation will certainly triumph. We must always be on the alert to feel the pulse of the movement and know the mood of the masses, estimate clearly the world situation and the situation in each period in order to seize the right opportunity and lead the masses of people to rise up in time ".

After the Japanese Coup d'Etat, in the historical instruction on March 12, 1945, the Party Central Committee clearsightedly estimated that the situation was offering many new favourable conditions, but " conditions for the insurrection are not yet ripe ". At the same time, it pointed out that when the Allied troops landed in Indo-China and the Japanese sent their troops to intercept them, thus exposing their rear, then would be the most favourable opportunity for launching the insurrection. The instruction added : *" If revolution breaks out and people's revolutionary power is set up in Japan, or if Japan is occupied as was France in 1940, and the Japanese expeditionary army demoralised, then, even if the Allied forces have not yet arrived in our country, our general insurrection can be launched and win victory".* The high tide of the revolution was sweeping throughout the country. The world situation changed rapidly. On August 8, 1945 the Soviet Red Army attacked in North-east China, and within a few days, the crack Japanese Kwantung Army was entirely routed. Japanese fascism was in an extremely critical situation and sought unconditional surrender. At that moment, the National Conference of the Party, which was being held at Tan Trao village, together with the Viet Minh General Committee, took a decision to order the launching of the General Insurrection and the setting up of people's power throughout the country. The National Insurrection Committee was established. After-wards, the National People's Congress held at Tan Trao set up the Viet Nam National Liberation Committee that was tantamount to the Provisional Government of the Democratic Republic of Viet Nam, headed by President Ho Chi Minh.

News of the Japanese capitulation spread rapidly. Having thoroughly understood the Party's instructions, and taking advantage of the extreme demoralisation of the Japanese forces, the consternation of the puppet government and the vacillation of the security troops, the local Party organisations and Viet Minh organisation immediately took the initiative to lead the people to seize power even before receiving the insurrection order. On August 11, insurrection broke out in Ha Tinh province ; on August 12, the insurrection order was proclaimed in the free zone, the Liberation army stormed many enemy's posts and a few days later marched to liberate Thai Nguyen. On August 13, the people in Quang Ngai province arose . On August 19, a splendid victory was scored by the insurrection in Hanoi Capital ; on August 23, the insurrection was successful in Hue, and on August 25, in Saigon. On August 29, the first unit of the Viet Nam Liberation Army entered the Capital city of Hanoi. Throughout the country, in town and countryside, millions of people rose up to wrest back power from the hands of the Japanese fascists and pro-Japanese puppets, shattering the fetters of the imperialists and feudalists. Basing ourselves on the powerful political forces of the people, backed by military and para-military forces, and on our skill in neutralising the Japanese army then in dismay, the insurrection cost little blood and rapidly gained success from North to South. In face of the people's powerful strength, Bao Dai abdicated, the Tran Trong Kim puppet government surrendered. On September 2, the Provisional Government appeared before the people. At historic Ba Dinh square, President Ho read the Declaration of Independence. The Democratic Republic of Viet Nam came into being, a great historical event of South-east Asia.

Availing itself of the right opportunity, our Party led the August General Insurrection to victory. Had the insurrection broken out sooner, it would have certainly met with numerous difficulties. It would have been in a dangerous situation had it broken out later, when the Chiang Kai-shek and British armies had arrived in our country. The Party led the people to seize power immediately after the Japanese capitulation and before the Allied forces arrived in Indo-China. The splendid victory of the insurrection was due to its timely launching.

The above-mentioned lessons were victories for the leadership of our Party, the subjective conditions leading the August General Insurrection to victory. Of course, the triumph of the August General Insurrection was also due to very important objective conditions. The great victory of the Soviet Red army and Allied forces over the German-Italian-Japanese fascists created favourable conditions for the liberation of the oppressed peoples in the world In our country, during the days of the August Insurrection, the enemy of the revolution was brought to an utter crisis. After France was occupied by German troops, the French colonialists' forces and influence in our country grew markedly weaker. Then, due to acute contradictions between the competing invaders, the enemy who had ruled for long over our country was defeated by the Japanese. Consequently, the feudal administration set up by the French also disintegrated. After March 9, the Japanese fascists, the main enemy of our people, were in a critical stage due to successive failures. The pro-Japanese puppet government having no solid foundation, was not able to cope with the ever growing revolutionary movement. Following the great victory of the Soviet Red Army and the Japanese fascists' capitulation, the spirit of the Japanese army in Indo-China was brought to utter crisis, their dream of enslaving our country had shattered. In view of this situation, the revolutionary masses were able to neutralise the Japanese. Thanks to this, no fierce resistance was met with and the General Insurrection triumphed rapidly. The above-mentioned objective factors proved the great influence and assistance of the socialist, democratic and peaceful forces, particularly that of the Soviet Red Army's great victory, towards our revolution. It has proved that the Vietnamese revolution is part of the world socialist revolution, our era is the era of socialist revolution and national liberation revolution, an era of decay and disintegration of imperialism and colonialism. This important objective condition does not in any way belittle the Party's precise and clearsighted leadership and its effect on the success of the August General Insurrection. To realise the decisive role of correct leadership, suffice it to compare the situation of our country with that of a number of countries in South-east Asia at that time. In the same month of August and under the same favourable objective conditions, not only did the revolution in these countries not win great success but it even met with setbacks.

The August General Insurrection was a great victory for our people and our Party. *This was a successful uprising of the people of a colonial and semi-feudal country, under the leadership of the Communist Party. Through a long political struggle, it developed into a regional armed struggle in the pre-insurrectionary period. In the end, seizing the right opportunity, when the enemy was in utter crisis, and making use mainly of the masses' political forces with the support of the armed and semi-armed forces, we heroically rose in the cities and the countryside, smashed the rule of the imperialists and feudalists and set up people's democratic power. The success of the August General Insurrection proves that the liberation movement of the oppressed nations, in given historical conditions, can be victorious through insurrection.*

This was the first time the people in a weak and small colony gallantly rose up under the leadership of the Communist Party and freed themselves from the chains of the imperialists and their stooges. The August General Insurrection was a good contribution to the upsurge of the national liberation movement in the world which rose like a high tide in and after World War Two, foretelling the coming disintegration of colonialism.

II

OUR PARTY VICTORIOUSLY LED THE LONG-TERM RESISTANCE WAR AGAINST THE FRENCH IMPERIALISTS AND U.S. INTERVENTIONISTS

Soon after the victory of the August Revolution and the founding of the Democratic Republic of Viet Nam, assisted by the British forces, the French colonialists launched war and occupied Saigon on September 23, 1945, thus invading our country once more. Our Southern compatriots resolutely resisted. On December 19, 1946, the nation-wide Resistance War broke out. This was a long, hard and extremely heroic liberation war of our people against the French imperialists and the U.S. interventionists. This resistance was carried on for 9 years and ended with our great victory at Dien Bien Phu and at the Geneva Conference. Peace has been restored in Indo-China on the basis of respect of the sovereignty, independence, unity and territorial integrity of our country, Cambodia and Laos. The North of our country has been entirely liberated.

The successful nine years of Resistance are the most glorious pages in the history of our people in the process of mobilisation for national liberation. Under the Party leadership, our people, from the days they rose against the enemy in Nam Bo until the Dien Bien Phu victory, fought and defeated an aggressive army of a powerful imperialist country. In this article, we try to point out some essential experiences of our Party in leading the revolutionary war.

1. First of all, our resistance won victory because the Party's policy of uniting the entire people to resolutely wage the Resistance war was a correct policy.

As at the beginning of World War Two, the policy advanced by the Party was to prepare for armed uprising to liberate our country. In the years 1945-1946, immediately after the establishment of the democratic republican regime, the Party put forward the policy of uniting the entire people resolutely to wage the Resistance War to safeguard the achievements of the August Revolution and newly-recovered independence.

Following the success of the Revolution, the Party clearly realised the danger of aggression from the French colonialists. Even in the Declaration of Independence and in the Oath of Independence, the Party called for a heightening of vigilance, and mobilised the people to be prepared to defend the Fatherland.

The French colonialists' aggressive war broke out in Saigon when people's power had not yet been consolidated and great difficulties in all fields lay ahead of us. Never had our country borne the yoke of so many foreign armies. The Japanese had capitulated but were still in possession of their arms. The Chiang Kai-shek army which landed in the North, did its best to assist the Viet Nam Quoc Dan Dang * to overthrow people's power In the South, British forces occupied the country up to the 16th parallel and tried to help the French colonialists expand their aggressive war.

Our Party led the people in Nam Bo to wage a resistance war against the French colonialists. To spearhead all its forces at the principal enemy, the Party carried out the line of winning more friends and less enemies, endeavoured to widen the national united front, founded the Viet Nam National United Front (called Lien Viet for short), united all forces which could be united, neutralised all those which could be neutralised and differentiated between forces which could be differentiated. At the same time, it consolidated power, developed and consolidated the armed forces, elected the National Assembly and formed the Government of coalition for the Resistance.

In its foreign policy, our Party tried by every means to realise a cordial policy with the Chiang Kai-shek army and avoid all conflicts. Dealing with the main enemy, the French aggressive colonialists, on the one hand, our Party led the people and army in Nam Bo resolutely to resist against their aggressive army, mobilised the entire people throughout the country to do their best in supporting the South, sent troops there and at the same time actively prepared for the resistance in case the war spread out. On the other hand, it did not miss any opportunity to take advantage of the contradictions between the French and Chiang Kai-shek forces and to negotiate with the French Government to secure a detente and preserve peace.

---

* The Vietnamese Kuomintang

The signing of the Preliminary Convention on March 6, 1946 between the French and our forces was the result of this correct policy and strategy. Due to the concession granted by us, part of the French army could land at certain localities in north Viet Nam to relieve the Chiang troops. On the French Government's side, it recognised that the Democratic Republic of Viet Nam was a free country within the framework of the French Union, having its own government, army, parliament, finance, etc.. Thus, we succeeded in driving 200,000 Chiang Kai-shek troops out of our country. Following this, the counter-revolutionary army of the Viet Nam Quoc Dan Dang which still occupied 5 provinces along the frontier and the Midland of north Viet Nam was also annihilated. The democratic republican regime grew stronger.

With the Preliminary Convention, we had carried out the policy of " making peace to go forward ". Immediately after the signing of the Convention, there was a time when illusions of peace partly influenced our vigilance towards the colonialists' reactionary schemes. But in general, the Party kept on making efforts to consolidate peace, while increasing our forces, ready to cope with all the enemy's plots. On the one hand, it adhered the convention which had been signed, on the other hand, it resolutely carried out a self-defence struggle against all enemy acts sabotaging this convention. The French colonialists' schemes were revealed with every passing day. The more concessions we made, the further they trespassed. They openly tore the convention they had signed, carried on mopping-up operations in the provisionally occupied areas in the South, indulged in provocative acts, step by step encroached upon our rights in numerous localities including Haiphong, and

Hanoi Capital. They did their utmost to occupy our country. Therefore, when realising that all possibilities for maintaining peace no longer existed, the Party called on the entire people to wage the Resistance War.

Realities clearly showed the people that our Party and Government had done their utmost to maintain the policy of peace, but the French colonialists were determined to invade our country once more. It was obvious that there was no other way for our nation but to take up arms resolutely to safeguard the Fatherland. Practical deeds had clearly shown to the French people and peace-loving peoples all over the world that we wished to live in peace, but the French colonialists determinedly provoked war. That is why our people's War of Resistance won ever greater sympathy and support from the broad masses in France and the world over.

Our Party's policy of resistance was a precise one, in conformity with the masses' requirements, whose wrath towards the aggressors had reached a climax. For this very reason, in response to President Ho's appeal for carrying out a resistance war, our army and people did not shun hardships and sacrifices. Like one man, they were determined to wage the War of Resistance to final victory and annihilate the aggressors.

2. Throughout the resistance war, our Party fundamentally stuck firmly to the national democratic revolution line, therefore succeeded in launching the people's war and defeating the enemy

The Resistance War waged by our people was the continuation of the national democratic revolution by armed struggle. Therefore, to hold firm the national democratic revolution line in leading the Resistance War was a nodal, decisive question.

As is said above, Viet Nam was originally a colonial and semi-feudal country. Our society underwent great changes as a result of the August Revolution. Imperialist rule had been overthrown. The power of the king and mandarins, the imperialists' stooges representing the most reactionary section of the feudal landlord class had been overthrown. However, this class still existed in our society and the land question was only partly solved.

French colonial troops re-kindled the aggressive war. The basic contradiction between our people and imperialism reappeared in the most acute form. Who was the aggressive enemy ? Obviously the French imperialists. At the beginning, owing to the fact that there were progressive elements in the French government and due to tactical necessity, we named as our enemy French reactionary colonialists. But later, especially from 1947 on, the French government definitely became reactionary, the aggressors were unmistakably the French imperialists who were the enemy of our entire people and were invading our country. In this situation, the national factor was of utmost importance. To fight French imperialism, it was necessary to unite the whole nation, all revolutionary classes, patriotic elements, to strengthen and widen the National United Front. Our Party obtained great success in its policy of uniting the people. The slogan: "Unity, unity and broad unity — success, success and great success," put forth by President Ho Chi Minh became a great reality. The anti-imperialist National United Front in our country was a model of the broadest national front in a colonial country.

The revolution for national liberation under the leadership of the Communist Party never deviated from the democratic revolution. The anti-imperialist task always went side by side with the anti-feudal task, although the former was the more urgent; Viet Nam was a backward agricultural country and the great majority of the population were peasants. While the working class is the class leading the revolution, the peasantry is the main force of the revolution, full of anti-imperialist and anti-feudal spirit. Moreover, in waging the Resistance War, we relied on the countryside to build our bases to launch guerilla warfare in order to encircle the enemy in the towns and eventually arrive at liberating the towns. Therefore, it was of particularly importance to pay due attention to the peasant question and the anti-feudal question to step up the long Resistance War to victory.

How did our Party solve the anti-feudal question with a view to mobilising the peasant force during the Resistance War? In the August Revolution, after we had overthrown the power of the king and mandarins, a number of traitors were punished, their land allotted to the peasants. Colonialists' land was also temporarily given to the peasants. After the French imperialists re-invaded our country, the collusion between the imperialists and the most reactionary section of the feudal landlord class gradually took shape.

The essential contradiction in our society at that time was the contradiction between, on the one side, our nation, our people, and on the other, the French imperialists and their henchmen, the reactionary feudalists. We accordingly put forth the slogan " To exterminate the reactionary colonialists and the traitors." As a result, as early as the first years of the Resistance War, a number of the most reactionary of the landlord class were repressed in the course of the operations against local puppet administration and traitors. Their land and that belonging to absent landlords were allotted outright or given to the trusteeship of the peasants. Thus, in practice, the anti-feudal task was carried on.

However, due to a vague conception of the content of the revolution for national liberation as early as 1941, in the first years of the Resistance War, in our mind as well as in our policies, the anti-feudal task was somewhat neglected and the peasant question underestimated in importance. Only by 1949 - 1950 was this question put in a more definite way. In 1952 - 1953, our Party decided to mobilise the masses for a drastic reduction of land rent and to carry out land reform, implementing the slogan "land to the tiller". Hence, the resistance spirit of millions of peasants was strongly roused, the peasant-worker alliance strengthened, the National United Front made firmer, the administration and army consolidated and resistance activities intensified. There were errors in land reform but they were, in the main, committed after the restoration of peace and thus did not have any effect on the Resistance War. It should be added that not only was land reform carried out in the North, but in south Viet Nam, land was also distributed to the peasants after 1951.

The carrying out of land reform during the Resistance War was an accurate policy of a creative character of our Party.

Looking back, on the whole, our Party stuck to the national democratic revolution line throughout the Resistance War. Thanks to this, we succeeded in mobilizing our people *to launch the people's war*, using the enormous strength of the people to vanquish the aggressors.

Right at the outbreak of the nation-wide Resistance War, the Party issued instructions for a *"whole nation Resistance War, all-out Resistance War"*. This was the fundamental content of the people's war. Through the struggles of the Resistance years, this content became richer and more concrete, especially after the launching of the guerilla war and after the peasant question was duly considered concurrently with the national question.

As the political objective of the Resistance War was national independence and land, and as this was in conformity with their deep and fundamental aspirations, the people arose to exterminate the aggressors and save the country. President Ho Chi Minh appealed: "All Vietnamese regardless of sex, age, creed, political tendency and nationality must stand up to fight the French colonialists and save the country. Those who have guns use guns, those who have swords use swords, and those who have no swords use picks, shovels or sticks. Everyone has to do his utmost against the colonialists to save the country." The Vietnamese people responded to President Ho Chi Minh's call and millions rose as one man to wage the Resistance War, annihilate the enemy and save the country. This people's war was, from the point of view of forces, mainly a peasants' war. The peasants had for a long time fought under the Party's banner, rosed up to seize the power in the August Revolution, and throughout the long and hard Resistance War also played a great and important part.

In fact, our Resistance War was a people's war. On the battlefronts the armymen rushed forward to annihilate the enemy, while in the rear the people were striving to increase production — the peasants in the fields and the workers in the arms-factories — in order to supply the troops, to serve the front line. The people's armed forces were the regular army and the regional troops and guerilla units. With the slogan " the whole nation in arms " each person was a soldier, each village a fortress, each Party branch and Resistance committee a staff. It was so in the free zones and all the more so in the enemy-occupied zones.

Our people's Resistance War was an all-out Resistance War. Not only did we fight in the military field but also in the political, economic and cultural fields. In the political field, we had, at home, to increase the education and mobilisation of the people, unremittingly strengthen national solidarity and endeavour to smash all the enemy's schemes to divide and deceive our people, while in its foreign policy, efforts had to be made to win over the support of progressive people throughout the world, particularly to closely co-ordinate with the struggle of the French people and those in the French colonies against this dirty war. In the economic field, great efforts had to be made to build a Resistance War economy, increase production, realise self-reliance and self-sufficiency in order to perseveringly wage the long Resistance War ; at the same time we had to do our utmost to sabotage the enemy's economy, to frustrate his plots to grab our manpower and wealth, to " use war to feed war ". In the cultural field, we had to develop the culture of the Resistance imbued with a mass character and to heighten patriotism and hatred. Simultaneously, we had to actively struggle to wipe out the influence of obscurantist culture in the free zones, to fight against the enemy's debased culture in the occupied zones, to break to pieces the enemy's counter-propaganda, to maintain and raise the confidence and determination to carry on the Resistance War of the whole people.

Under the Party's leadership, the people's administration played an important part in the mobilisation of manpower and wealth for the Resistance. " All for the front, all for victory " was the slogan for our nation and it showed the determination of our people to concentrate all their forces to fight to the bitter end to overthrow the French imperialists and their henchmen, liberate the country and wrest back independence and land. This was the slogan of the people's war.

3. Our Party put forth the correct strategic guiding principle: long-term resistance war, self-reliance, and the appropriate fighting principle: guerilla warfare and eventually advancing to mobile warfare.

Launching the Resistance War, our Party accurately assessed the strong and weak points of the enemy and ours and clearly saw the balance of forces and the enemy strategic schemes in order to define our strategic principle.

The *enemy*, an imperialist power much weakened after World War Two, was still strong as compared with us. Moreover, he possessed a seasoned professional army equipped with up-to-date arms, well supplied and experienced in aggressive wars. His weak point lay in the unjust character of his war. As a result, he was internally divided, not supported by the people of his own country and did not enjoy the sympathy of world opinion. His army was strong at the beginning but its fighting spirit was deteriorating. French imperialism had other weak points and difficulties, namely : limited manpower and wealth, their dirty war was strongly condemned by their countrymen, etc.

On *our side*, our country was originally a colonial and semi-feudal country whose independence was newly won back. Thus, our forces in all fields were not yet consolidated, our economy was a backward agrarian one, our army untried guerilla troops with few and obsolete arms, our supplies insufficient and our cadres lacking experiences. Our strong point lay in the just nature of our Resistance War. Hence, we succeeded in uniting our entire people. Our people and troops were always imbued with the spirit of sacrificing themselves in fighting the enemy, and enjoyed the sympathy and support of people throughout the world.

These were the main features of the two sides in the last Resistance War. They clearly pointed out that the enemy's strong points were his weak ones and our strong points were his weak ones, but the enemy's strong points were temporary ones while ours were basic ones.

Owing to the above-mentioned characteristics, *the enemy's strategic principle was to attack swiftly and win swiftly*. The more the war was protracted the lesser would be his strong points, and their weak points would grew weaker. This strategic principle was in contradiction with the French imperialists' limited forces which had grown much weaker after World War Two. Consequently, in their schemes of invading our country, they were compelled to combine their plan of attacking swiftly and win swiftly with that of invading step-by-step, and even of negotiating with us in their time-serving policy to muster additional forces. Despite the difficulties and obstacles caused by their weak points, whenever they had the possibility, they would immediately carry out their plan of attacking swiftly and winning swiftly, hoping to end the war by a quick victory. From the very beginning of the war, French colonialists had the ambition to complete their occupation and " pacification " of south Viet Nam within a few weeks. The nation-wide Resistance War broke out. On the failure of their attempt to wipe out our main forces in the cities, they did their utmost to regroup their troops and launched a big offensive in Viet Bac, expecting to annihilate our leading organs and main forces in order to score a decisive success. The offensive in Viet Bac was brought to failure, the enemy was forced to protract the war and switch over to " pacifying" the areas in his rear but he had not as yet given up his strategic plan of attacking swiftly and winning swiftly. The reshuffling of generals time and again, especially the sending of General Navarre to Indo-China were all aimed at striking decisive blows in order to quickly end the aggressive war.

Realising clearly the enemy's strong and weak points and ours, to cope with the enemy's strategic scheme, *our Party set forth the guiding principle of a long-term Resistance War.* Facing an enemy who temporarily had the upper hand, our people was not able to strike swiftly and win swiftly but needed time to overcome its shortcomings and increase the enemy's weak points. Time was needed to mobilise, organise and foster the forces of the Resistance, to wear out the enemy forces, gradually reverse the balance of forces, turning our weakness into strength and concurrently availing ourselves of the changes in the international situation which was growing more and more avantageous to our Resistance, eventually to triumph over the enemy.

The general law of a long revolutionary war is usually to go through three stages: defensive, equilibrium and offensive. Fundamentally, in the main directions, our Resistance War also followed this general law. Of course, the reality on the battlefields unfolded in a more lively and more complicated manner. Implementing the guiding principle of a long war, after a period of fighting to wear out and check the enemy troops, we carried out a strategic withdrawal from the cities to the countryside in order to preserve our forces and defend our rural bases. Following the failure of the enemy offensive in Viet Bac, equilibrium gradually came into being. We decided to launch an extensive guerilla war. From 1950 onwards, campaigns of local counter-offensives were successively opened and we won the initiative on the northern battlefront. The Dien Bien Phu campaign in early 1954 was a big counter-offensive which ended the Resistance War with a great victory.

To make everyone thoroughly understand the strategic guiding principle of long-term war was not only a big work of organisation militarily and economically but also a process of ideological education and struggle within the Party and among the people against erroneous tendencies which appeared many a time in the years of the Resistance War. These were pessimistic defeatism which presumed that our country being small, our population thin, our economy backward and our armed forces young and weak, we would be unable to face the enemy, let alone perseveringly to wage a long Resistance War. These were subjectivism, loss of patience, eagerness to win swiftly which came out in the plans of operations of a number of localities at the start of the Resistance War which were unwilling to withdraw their force to preserve our main force, and in their plan of general counter-offensive put forth in 1950 when this was not yet permitted by objective and subjective conditions.

Utmost efforts were made by the Party to correct these erroneous tendencies, to educate the people, enabling them to see clearly our difficulties and advantages and stimulate the entire people to keep firm their determination to fight. The booklet *The Resistance War Will Win* written by comrade Truong Chinh was an important contribution to the thorough understanding of the Resistance War line and policies of the Party. Here, emphasis should be laid upon the great effect of the resolutions of the First Session of the Central Committee in 1951 which reminded the whole Party that "our Resistance War is a long and hard struggle" and "we have mainly to rely on our own forces". The ideological remoulding drives in the Party and the army and the propaganda work among the people carried out on the Central Committee's instructions, basically consolidated the people's determination to wage the long Resistance War, heightened their confidence in final victory and enabled the guiding principles of long-term and self-relying Resistance War to penetrate more deeply into the masses' consciousness.

To wage a long Resistance War, we had to highlight the spirit of *self-reliance*. During the first years of the Resistance, our people had to struggle when encircled on all sides, self-reliance was then a vital question. Our people had no other way than relying on their own forces to cope with the enemy. Highlighting the spirit of self-reliance, our troops looked for their supplies on the battlefields, capturing the enemy weapons to arm themselves, economising in munitions, developing their endurance, overcoming difficulties, striving to take part in production, supplying themselves with a part of their requirements, in order to lighten the people's contributions. Our people endeavoured to build our rear, develop the economy of the Resistance to supply themselves and meet the demand of the front. We stepped up production in every aspect to supply the people with staple commodities and fought against the enemy's economic blockade. Large areas of virgin land were broken to increase the output of foodstuffs. Many arms factories were built to produce weapons for the troops. In particular, the people and troops in the Fifth zone and Nam Bo raised to great heights the spirit of self-reliance, scored many achievements in self-supply to perseveringly wage the Resistance War in extremely difficult and hard circumstances.

When the international situation changed to our advantage, but we were still meeting with many difficulties, there began to appear in the Party and among the people the psychology of waiting and relying on foreign aid. Therefore, while continuing to ideologically prepare for a long Resistance War, attention was given by our Party to rousing our self-reliance and pointing out that international sympathy and support was of importance, but only by relying on our own efforts could we ensure victory for our people's struggle for liberation.

To bring the Resistance War to victory, it was not enough to have a correct strategic guiding principle but an appropriate *guiding principle of fighting* was also necessary in order successfully to carry out that strategic guiding principle. In general, our Resistance War was a *guerilla war moving gradually to regular war, from guerilla warfare to mobile warfare combined with partial entrenched camp warfare.* Basically, we had grasped that general law hence we were successful. However, we did not thoroughly grasp it from the beginning but only after a whole process of being tested and tempered in the practice of war.

In the Resistance War, *guerilla warfare* played an extremely important role. Guerilla warfare is the form of fighting of the masses of people, of the people of a weak and badly equipped country who stand up against an aggressive army which possesses better equipment and technique. This is the way of fighting the revolutionary war which relies on the heroic spirit to triumph over modern weapons, avoiding the enemy when he is the stronger and attacking him when he is the weaker, now scattering, now regrouping one's forces, now wearing out, now exterminating the enemy, determined to fight him everywhere, so that wherever the enemy goes he would be submerged in a sea of armed people who hit back at him, thus undermining his spirit and exhausting his forces. In addition to the units which have to be scattered in order to wear out the enemy, it is necessary to regroup big armed forces in favourable conditions in order to achieve supremacy in attack at a given point and at a given time to annihilate the enemy. Successes in many small fights added together gradually wear out the enemy manpower while little by little fostering our forces. The main goal of the fighting must be destruction of enemy manpower, and ours should not be exhausted from trying to keep or occupy land, thus creating final conditions to wipe out the whole enemy forces and liberate our country.

Guerilla warfare was obviously a form of fighting in full keeping with the characteristics of our Resistance War.

In the early period of the Resistance, there was not and could not be in our country regular war but only guerilla activities. When the Resistance War started in south Viet Nam, our plan was to wage guerilla warfare, and in practice guerilla war took shape. But when the nation-wide Resistance War broke out, the policy of mainly waging guerilla warfare was not clearly put forth. At the beginning of Autumn-Winter 1947, the Party Central Committee put forth the task of launching and extending guerilla activities all over the occupied areas. One part of our main force was divided into independent companies operating separately which penetrated deep into the enemy's rear-line to carry out propaganda among the people, defend our bases and intensify guerilla war. The policy of independent companies concurrently with concentrated battalions was a very successful experience in the direction of guerilla war. As guerilla activities were intensified and widely extended, many enemy's rear-lines were turned into our frontlines.

To cope with our ever-expanding guerilla activities, great efforts were made by the enemy to launch repeated mopping-up operations with ever-bigger armed forces. The aim of these operations was to annihilate our guerilla units, destroy our political bases and crops, and plunder our property, hoping to crush our resistance forces and "pacify" his rear. That is why mopping-up operation and counter mopping-up operation became the chief form of guerilla war in the enemy's rear-line. Through the counter mopping-up operations, our people brought to the utmost their endurance of hardships and heroic fighting spirit, creating extremely rich forms of fighting. To maintain and extend guerilla activities in the enemy's rear, our Party cleverly combined the co-ordination of political and economic struggle with armed struggle. The Party strove hard to avail itself of the favourable opportunities to push the people forward to the armed struggle, develop our forces, annihilate and wear out the enemy forces, turn temporarily occupied zones into guerilla zones or the latter into our bases. When meeting with a difficult situation, our Party cleverly switched the movement in good time to preserve our forces and safeguard our bases. Guerilla activities in the enemy's rear were the highest expression of the iron will and extremely courageous spirit of our people, and at the same time a proof of the talented leadership of the Party.

From the strategic point of view, guerilla warfare, causing many difficulties and losses to the enemy, wears him out. To annihilate big enemy manpower and liberate land, guerilla warfare has to move gradually to *mobile warfare*. As our Resistance War was a long revolutionary war, therefore guerilla warfare not only could but had to move to mobile warfare. Through guerilla activities, our troops were gradually formed, fighting first with small units then with bigger ones, moving from scattered fighting to more concentrated fighting. Guerilla warfare gradually developed to mobile warfare — a form of fighting in which principles of regular warfare gradually appear and increasingly develop but still bear a guerilla character. Mobile warfare is the fighting way of concentrated troops, of the regular army in which relatively big forces are regrouped and operating on a relatively vast battlefield, attacking the enemy where he is relatively exposed with a view to annihilating enemy manpower, advancing very deeply then withdrawing very swiftly, possessing to the extreme, dynamism, initiative, mobility and rapidity of decision in face of new situations. As the Resistance War went on, the strategic role of mobile warfare became more important with every passing day. Its task was to annihilate a bigger and bigger number of the enemy forces in order to develop our own, while the task of guerilla warfare was to wear out and destroy the enemy's reserves. Therefore, mobile warfare had to go side by side with annihilating warfare. Only by annihilating the enemy's manpower, could we smash the enemy's big offensives, safeguard our bases and our rear-line, move to win the initiative in the operations, wipe out more and more important enemy manpower, liberating larger and larger localities one after the other and eventually arrive at destroying the whole enemy armed forces and liberating our whole country.

Implementing the guiding principle of moving gradually from guerilla warfare to mobile warfare, from the outset, there was in our guerilla troops, besides one part operating separately, another with concentrated activity, and this was the first seeds of mobile warfare. In 1947, with the plan of independent companies operating separately and concentrated battalions, we began to move to more concentrated fighting, then to mobile warfare. In 1948, we made relatively great ambuscades and surprise attacks with one or several battalions. In 1949, we launched small campaigns not only in the North but also on other battlefronts. From 1950, we began to launch campaigns on an ever larger scale enabling mobile warfare to play the main part on the northern battlefield, while entrenched camp warfare was on the upgrade. This fact was clearly manifest in the great Dien Bien Phu campaign.

We used to say: guerilla war must multiply. To keep itself in life and develop, guerilla warfare has necessarily to develop into mobile warfare. This is a general law. In the concrete conditions of our Resistance War, there could not be mobile warfare without guerilla warfare. But if guerilla warfare did not move to mobile warfare, not only the strategic task of annihilating the enemy manpower could not be carried out but even guerilla activities could not be maintained and extended. To say that it is necessary to develop guerilla warfare into mobile warfare does not mean brushing aside guerilla warfare, but that in the widely extended guerilla activities, the units of the regular army gradually grew up and were able to wage mobile warfare and side by side with that main force there must always be numerous guerilla troops and guerilla activities.

Once mobile warfare appeared on the battlefront of guerilla war, there must be close and correct co-ordination between these forms of fighting to be able to step up the Resistance War, wear out and annihilate bigger enemy forces and win ever greater victories. This is another general law in the conduct of the war. On the one hand, guerilla warfare had to be extended to make full use of the new favourable conditions brought about by mobile warfare, in order to co-ordinate with mobile warfare to wear out and annihilate a great number of enemy manpower and through these successes continue to step up mobile warfare. On the other hand, mobile warfare had to be accelerated to annihilate big enemy manpower, and concurrently create new favourable conditions for a further extension of guerilla warfare. In the course of the development of mobile warfare, owing to the enemy's situation and ours on the battlefields, entrenched camp warfare gradually came into being. Entrenched camp warfare which became part and parcel of the mobile warfare, kept developing and occupied a more and more important position.

The conduct of the war must maintain a correct ratio between the fighting forms. At the beginning, we had to stick to guerilla warfare and extend it. Passing to a new stage, as mobile warfare made its appearance, we had to hold firm the co-ordination between the two forms, the chief one being guerilla warfare ; mobile warfare was of lesser importance but was on the upgrade. Then came a new and higher stage, mobile warfare moved to the main position, at first, only on one battlefield — local counter-offensive came into being — then on an ever wider scope. During this time, guerilla warfare extended but, contrary to mobile warfare, it moved back from the main position to a lesser but still important one, first on a given battle-front then on an ever-wider scope.

In the practice of the liberation war, on some battle-fronts we met with numerous difficulties because we were not determined to advance guerilla warfare to mobile warfare ; on others, rashness in speeding up mobile warfare had a bad influence on guerilla warfare, and therefore mobile warfare also met with difficulties. This manifes-tation was relatively widespread when the slogan "To prepare for the general counter-offensive" was put forth, but it was overcome after a certain time. In general, through tests and trials, our guidance fundamentally held firm the aforesaid ratio and was therefore successful. The Hoa Binh campaign was typical of co-ordination between guerilla warfare and mobile warfare on the northern battle-front. The Dien Bien Phu campaign and Winter-Spring 1953 — 1954 campaign were most successful models of co-ordination between mobile warfare and guerilla warfare, between the face to face battlefield and the theatres of operation in the enemy's rear, between the main battle-field and the co-ordinated battlefields all over the country.

With the forms of guerilla fighting and mobile fighting and owing to the enemy's conditions and ours in strength, shaping up of force and topography, etc., there appeared on the battlefronts the situation of free zones interlacing with enemy-controlled areas, intersecting and encircling each other. In the enemy-controlled areas, there were also guerilla zones and guerilla bases, another phenomenon of interlacement, intersecting and encircling one another. The process of development of the war was that of ever-widening of our free zones and guerilla areas and ever-narrowing of the enemy-occupied areas, advancing towards liberating vast areas, then the whole North.

The strategy of long-term war and the guiding principle of fighting from guerilla war gradually moving to regular war with the forms of guerilla warfare, mobile warfare including entrenched camp warfare, were very success-ful experiences of our national liberation war. These were the strategy and tactics of the people's war, the art of military conduct of the people's war, of the revolutionary war in a small and backward agricultural country under the leadership of our Party.

In the course of the national liberation war, *the build-ing of bases* for a steadfast and long resistance was an important strategic question and also a very successful ex-perience of our Party. It is an absolute necessity for us to make a profound study of and to sum up the rich experien-ces of this question.

* *
*

The success of the Vietnamese Resistance War was the success of the people of a country which was originally a colonial and semi-feudal country with a small area, a small population, and an extremely backward agricultural economy, which, under the leadership of the vanguard party of the working class, rose up to wage a long armed struggle against an aggressive imperialist country.

The successful Resistance War has completely liberated the North. For the first time in nearly one hundred years in modern history, the shadows of an imperialist enemy and colonial soldiers are no longer seen on a half of our country. The successful Resistance War has brought about conditions for the drastic completion of land reform. After thousands of years of feudal rule, the system of exploitation of the landlord class has been abolished once for all over a half of our country. The victorious Resistance War has created conditions for the revolution in the liberated North to move to the socialist stage. At present, economic restoration has been achieved, land reform completed, our people are striving to accelerate the socialist transformation and socialist construction turning the North into an ever-stronger base for the struggle to achieve national unification and continue to complete the national democratic revolution throughout the country.

The sacred Resistance War of our people has continued the glorious work of the August Revolution, raising aloft the banner of national liberation against colonialism and has eloquently proved that : " *In the present international conditions, even a weak and small nation, once united to stand up under the leadership of the working class, resolutely to struggle for independence and democracy, will have full capacity to defeat all aggressive forces. This struggle for national liberation, in given historical conditions can, through the form of a long-armed struggle — a long resistance war — come to success.''*

The successful Resistance War of our people has dealt a heavy blow to the ever-disintegrating colonialist system, thus contributing a part to the smashing of the imperialists' war-provoking plots, and to the struggle of the world people for peace, democracy and socialism.

To speak of the factors of victory in a more comprehensive way, the Resistance War of our people has obtained success thanks, first, to the leadership of the Party of the working class, second, to the fact that our Party has taken into due account the peasant question and organised the broad National United Front on the firm basis of the worker-peasant alliance, third, because we have a heroic people's army, fourth, because our State power genuinely belongs to the people, fifth, thanks to the solidarity and support of the people of the brother countries and peace-loving people in the world including the French people and those of the French colonies. Within the limit of this article, we do not analyse the causes of our success in an overall way, but we speak only of our Party's leadership to point out the great experiences in leadership.

OUR PARTY HAS SUCCESSFULLY LED THE BUILDING OF THE PEOPLE'S REVOLUTIONARY ARMED FORCES

In the decisive struggle to liberate the nation, overthrow imperialism and its henchmen, our people — first of all the worker-peasant masses — under our Party's leadership, stood up with arms in hand to build their own armed forces. Lenin says: " An oppressed class, if not making efforts to learn to wield arms and to obtain them, only deserves to be treated as slaves. "[1] Our people have learned to wield arms and have their own armed forces, therefore their work of liberation has scored success in half of the country. With the setting up of people's power, the building of the people's armed forces was all the more urgent. This was a task of utmost importance during the Resistance War and still is a very important task now, in peace time.

Our people's revolutionary armed forces were born in the revolutionary struggle of the entire people, first of all the broad worker-peasant masses. The first resolutions of our Party already posed the question of setting up worker-peasant self-defence units and the worker-peasant army. In the Nghe-Tinh Soviet movement, there appeared the Red

---

[1] V. Lenin · **Military Programme of the Proletarian Revolution**

Self-defence units which were the embryo of the revolutionary armed forces of the people under our Party's leadership.

During World War Two, when preparations for armed insurrection became the urgent task of the revolution, the self-defence and fighting self-defence forces again came into being and developed, first in the revolutionary bases in the Viet Bac mountain area, then in vast areas all over the country. The predecessors of the People's Army came into existence one after the other: the National Salvation Unit, the Viet Nam Liberation Armed Propaganda Unit, and the Ba To guerilla unit. These small troops fought very heroically, kept themselves in existence and developed in extremely difficult conditions when the enemy was hundreds of times stronger. With the anti-Japanese surging high tide in 1945, guerilla war was launched, people's power set up in the liberated zone and the revolutionary armed forces grouped under the name of Viet Nam Liberation Army. In the August General Insurrection, together with the people throughout the country, the Liberation Army and self-defence forces rose up to seize power. In the glorious days of August and after the success of the Revolution, the ranks of the Liberation Army extended very quickly and became the armed forces of the Democratic Republican State, that is the present Viet Nam People's Army. The above-mentioned years can be regarded as *the period of formation of our army.*

Through nine years of the Resistance War, the People's Army unremittingly fought against French imperialists and American interventionists. These nine years of heroic fighting and glorious victory were also the *period in which our army was tempered and grew up.* Our People's Army grew stronger with every passing day, going from one victory to another, and ended the Resistance War with the great Dien Bien Phu victory, contributing its part to the restoration of peace in Indo-China and the complete liberation of half of our country.

In the last five years, our army entered for the first time *the period of building in peace time*. Our army is speeding up every aspect of its building in peace time in order to become a powerful people's army so as to make of it a regular and modern army fulfilling its task of safeguarding the socialist revolution and construction in the North and serving as a support for the struggle to achieve national unification by peaceful means.

The Viet Nam People's Army is a revolutionary army which was born in the revolutionary movement of the people of a colony who arose to liberate themselves. Our army courageously fought the French-Japanese imperialists in the pre-insurrectional period, and together with the whole nation founded the revolutionary power, and defeated the mercenary aggressive troops of the French colonialists backed by U.S. imperialists. Our army has raised to great heights the undaunted spirit of the nation, the indomitable fighting spirit of our people, and is worthy of being the army of an heroic nation.

The success of the People's Army is the great success of our people and our Party. In the process of building and growing up of the army, the Party has always pointed out the nature and task of the army, and defined the principles of building the army politically and militarily. Thanks to that, it came into being from nought, growing from a small beginning to a bigger army, from weakness to strength and has gloriously vanquished the enemy and fulfilled its revolutionary task in the historical stages.

1. Our army was successful and mature because it is a people's army led by the Party

For what reason has our army, though still young, already an extremely glorious history, scored resounding feats of arms and contributed an important part to the success of the revolution of our entire people ? Because it is a people's army, led by our Party. The Party's leadership is the decisive factor of all the successes of our army.

Our army was born and has grown up in the revolutionary struggle of the entire people. It is the implement of the Party and the revolutionary State for the carrying out of the revolutionary struggle and class struggle. It embraces the elite of the revolutionary classes, of the people of all nationalities in Viet Nam, first and mainly the finest worker and peasant elements who have volunteered to fight to the bitter end for the interests of the country, of the toiling people and of the worker-peasant masses.

Therefore, *our army is a people's army, the army of the toiling people, essentially, of the workers and peasants and led by the Party of the working class*. It is the armed forces of the people's democratic State, which was formerly in essence, the worker-peasant dictatorship and is now the proletarian dictatorship. This is *the question of the revolutionary nature and class nature of our army*. This is the basic difference between the enemy's army and ours. This is the most fundamental question which must be thoroughly understood in any stage of the building of the army.

Owing to its class nature, our army, since its setting up, has always been faithful to the revolutionary cause of the Party and people. The revolutionary task of the Party and people is also the target of the army's efforts.

The working out of a correct *revolutionary line and task* has a decisive effect in the building of the armed forces. In the previous stage, our entire people was carrying out the national democratic revolution throughout the country, aimed at overthrowing imperialism and the feudal landlord class, winning national independence, bringing land to the peasants and creating conditions to advance the revolution in our country to the socialist stage. At that time, during the hard years of the armed struggle, our people's army fought very heroically to annihilate the aggressive army of imperialism and the traitors, its henchmen. However, in the first years of the Resistance War, although the anti-imperialist task was set out clearly, the anti-feudal task was not put forth in full keeping with its importance. As a result, the national spirit and consciousness of the army was heightened but its class consciousness was rather weak, thus having a bad influence on drawing a line between the enemy and us. Since the moment our Party paid attention to the anti-feudal task, especially since the mobilisation of the masses for rent reduction and land reform, not only broad peasant masses in the rear were ideologically roused but also our army — the great majority being peasants and very eager for land — also saw clearly and more fully its own fighting objective that it not only fights for national independence, but also to bring land to the peasants, and consequently its class consciousness and fighting spirit were raised markedly.

Since our people's revolutionary struggle has entered the new stage, the task of our entire people is to struggle for national reunification, to continue to complete the national democratic revolution throughout the country ; to endeavour to advance the North to socialism and build a peaceful, united, independent, democratic, prosperous and strong Viet Nam. Basing itself on this revolutionary task, our Party has set the people's army the political task of safeguarding the socialist building in the North to serve as the mainstay of the struggle for national unification and keeping itself ready to smash all aggressive plots of imperialism, mainly U.S. imperialism and its stooges. As the common revolutionary task and political task of the army are accurately set out, the political education in the army, especially the recent ideological remoulding class, having a precise and concrete direction, have raised to new heights the socialist consciousness and patriotism of all the officers and men, creating a new revolutionary mettle in the whole army that has been showing itself in the emulation movement to advance rapidly and overfulfil the plan with a view to making as great a contribution as possible to socialism. The army has seen more clearly its task with regard to the maintaining of social order in the North while the struggle between the two paths unfolds, as well as to the defence of territorial security.

Our army is made up of officers and men who are imbued with revolutionary consciousness and fighting spirit. It has a fine revolutionary nature. However, to say so does not mean that it is not necessary to strive to maintain and strengthen that class nature. On the contrary, in its leadership, the Party must pay *great attention to the question of maintaining and strengthening the revolutionary and class nature of our army.* Only by working out and thoroughly grasping the Party's revolutionary task in the army, only by strengthening without cease the Party's leadership and increasing political work, can we succeed in doing that, in enabling the army fulfil its own revolutionary task.

Since the restoration of peace, our Party has put forth the guiding principle of building a powerful people's army that will gradually become a regular and modern army. The question of maintaining the revolutionary nature of the army is still a fundamental demand of utmost importance. Only by maintaining and strengthening the revolutionary nature of the army and by raising its socialist consciousness and patriotism, can we succeed in turning it into a regular and modern army. On the way to become a regular and modern army, our army will always be a people's army. It must become a modern revolutionary army.

The Party's leadership is the decisive key question to enable the army to maintain its class nature and carry out its revolutionary task. The Party's leadership of the army is an absolute one. This leadership reveals itself politically: to imbue the army with the Party's revolutionary line in order to make of it the faithful implement of the Party in the carrying out of the revolutionary task. This leadership shows itself ideologically: to educate the army in the ideology of the working class, in Marxism-Leninism, to use Marxism-Leninism as the compass for all activities, as the one and only guiding ideology of our army. This leadership still reveals itself organisationally: to thoroughly understand the Party's class line in the building of the Party as well as in the work concerning the cadres in our army. Only by doing that can our army be always a genuine people's army which is ready to fulfil its own revolutionary task in all circumstances, thereby becoming more and more mature and winning new successes.

2. Our Party has correctly defined the fundamental principles of political building of the army

The most fundamental principle in the building of our army is to put it under the Party's leadership, *to ceeaselessly strengthen the Party's leadership* of the army. The Party is the founder, organiser and educator of the army. Only by realising the Party's absolute leadership can the army unswervingly follow the class line, the political direction and fulfil its own revolutionary task. To carry out and strengthen the Party's leadership *great attention must be given to the work of building the Party and political works, and the system of Party Committee and political commissar must be firmly maintained*. Only thanks to the firm organisation of the Party which serves as the core and leading nucleus in the army can the Party, through its own organisation — from Party committees down to Party branches — guide the implementation of its line and policies. Here stress should be laid on the important role of the grass-root Party branch; only when it is strong can the company be strong. The method of Party committee taking the lead, and the commander allotting the work coupled with the regime of political commissar, ensures the carrying out of the principle of collective leadership. It thereby succeeds in concentrating the knowledge of many people and also consolidating the solidarity based on ideological unity, closely co-ordinating the various tasks in the army, uniting the mind and deeds and increasing the army's fighting strength. Here, we have to emphasise that the method of Party committee taking the lead must always be coupled with the method of the commander allotting the work, in line with the Party's principle of collective leadership and personal responsibility. Political work is Party work and work of mass mobilisation of the Party in the army. Political work is the soul, the sinews of the army. Political work takes care of the building of the Party, guides the education of the army in the ideas of Marxism-Leninism, in the revolutionary line and task of the Party, military line and task of the Party, ensures good relations between officers and men, between the army and the people, between the army and the State, between our army and the armies and people of the brother countries and enables our army to have a high combativeness capable of defeating all enemies.

Right at the founding of our army, the first armed groups and platoons had their Party groups and branches. The platoons had their political commissars. On coming into being, the regiments had political commissars. The method of Party committee taking the lead and the commander allotting the work also took shape from the very first days. Officers were provided with hand-books *The Political Commissar's book* or *Political Work in the Army*. After the August Revolution, the traditional method of Party's leadership and political work was basically kept up, but in the first years, there appeared the tendency of not taking into due account the part played by political work and political work did not yet grasp that the main task was political education and ideological leadership. Sometimes, the Party's political agitation in the army was not closely co-ordinated with the Party work. After the Second Party Congress, the Party's leadership was strengthened in the army as in all other branches of activity. Agitation for ideological remoulding courses in the Party and the army, brought about increased education on the long-term war and self-relying war of resistance, education in policies, mobilisation of the masses for drastic reduction of land rent and land reform. Political work in the army became richer and more concrete, thus its position was markedly raised and its strength grew visibly. The Party's leadership was consolidated. Political work had a great effect on the raising of the ideological level, educating and consolidating the class stand of officers and men. It had a great effect, a lively content full of combativeness and mass character, in our big military campaigns as well as in guerilla war on all battlefronts.

Since the restoration of peace, in the new revolutionary stage, the Party's leadership and work of consolidating and developing the Party has been carried on steadily. Through congresses of Party delegates from all echelons, inner-Party democracy was implemented and the role of the Party branches highlighted. The ideological remoulding courses which set out a clear line — strengthen solidarity, raise to new heights the fighting spirit and socialist consciousness. Especially, the ideological remoulding drive last year which aimed at thoroughly grasping the resolutions of the Party Central Committee on the revolutionary task and line of the people's war and people's army, achieved good results and contributed to the strengthening of our army's revolutionary nature. Attention was also given to education on Marxism-Leninism. Entering a new stage, and faced with the urgent demand of turning our army into a regular and modern one, in some works there appeared to a certain degree the tendency to disregard political work. When dealing with the necessity to strengthen centralisation and unification, although this principle was not yet sufficiently implemented, there appeared the tendency to slight the role of the Party branches and collective leadership of the Party committees. When dealing with the necessity to strengthen the material and technical bases in the army, to master technology, although the technical level of our army is still low and needs to be raised further, there emerged the tendency to belittle the role of politics, to divorce politics from technology, from specialisation, falling into the bourgeois viewpoint of pure militarism and technology. In the last ideological remoulding drive, these erroneous tendencies were corrected in the main. From now on, we still have to continue to strengthen political education and ideological leadership in the army, continue educating and fostering socialist ideology and patriotism, energetically combating all the expressions of bourgeois and other non-proletarian ideologies, fighting individualism and liberalism, thereby to maintain and constantly raise the solidarity and combativeness of our army.

Our army is made up of combatants who consciously fight for the revolutionary cause of the people, therefore our officers and men are completely single-minded about their fighting objective and class interest. We must always take care *to strengthen the monolithic solidarity within the army.* The relation between the officers and soldiers, between the higher and lower echelons, between one branch and another. is the relation of solidarity between comrades based on political equality and class love. This relation has been built up from the very founding of the army. Through the long

years of fighting in hard conditions of dangers and privations, our officers and men have loved each other like blood
brothers, sharing hardships and joys together, united for life
and in death. Concurrently with the raising of their class
consciousness, the solidarity between officers and men has
been more and more strengthened. This unity has welded
all the members of our army into an unbreakable monolithic
block.

Up till now, in general the question of internal unity
has always been taken into consideration and has become a
fine tradition of our army. However, in entering the new
stage of building the army, in a number of units and
organs, internal unity has not been taken into due account.
To strengthen the regular management and set up organisations are of utmost necessity, but in the actual task of
turning the army into a regular army, beside correct measures, there were bothersome and unnecessary provisions on
certain privileges which kept the officers apart from the
soldiers, the higher from the lower echelons, having some
bad effect on the comradeship and solidarity in the army.
These mistakes were corrected in good time.

Our army is a revolutionary army belonging to the
people and fighting under the Party's leadership, therefore
the interests of the army and the people are one and
the same. We must always take care to *strengthen the
monolithic solidarity between the army and the people*. The
army and the people are of the same heart, they are like
fish and water. Our army has no other interests than
those of the people, of the toiling people and the worker-
peasant masses. Right from its inception, the question of
single-mindedness between the army and the people has
been laid down clearly in the ten-point pledge of honour

124

and 12 points of discipline in its relations with the people. During the Resistance War, not only did our army make sacrifices and struggle for the defence of national independence and the protection of the people's lives and property, doing nothing to the detriment of the people, but it also did its utmost to give the people a helpful hand in all their activities. Side by side with the people, our army made sacrifices and fought in the Resistance War to defeat the enemy of the nation, won national independence, enthusiastically struggled for land reform to overthrow the feudal landlord class and bring land to the peasants. As a result, the solidarity between the army and the people grew stronger, and the people trusted, loved and supported the army, taking care of them as of their own children. Since the restoration of peace, the traditional unity between the army and the people has been maintained and developed. After many years of fighting against the cruel enemy for national liberation, our combatants are still working tirelessly. On the one hand, they stand ready for the defence of the people's peaceful labour and on the other, they strive to intensify the work of mobilising the people and have never spared themselves when the people are in need of help. Our army has actively taken part in stepping up agricultural co-operation as it did formerly in land reform. Through the struggle against famine, drought and flood and the building of construction sites and factories, etc., it has shown itself a faithful servant of the people, as President Ho Chi Minh has always reminded it. In recent years, in response to the Party's call, tens of thousands of officers and men volunteered to go to remote areas on the frontier to break virgin land, set up army farms to accelerate the socialist construction of the Fatherland. As our armymen are the brothers and sons of the labouring people, in their relations with the people, we must hold firm the class viewpoint, and endeavour to strehgthen the solidarity between the army and the people, first of all, the worker-peasant masses. The army is regarded as an integral part of the working class, therefore its good relations with the people and the peasant masses have a great political significance. These express the political nature of the officers and men of our army, showing clearly that it is not only a fighting army but also a working army. At present, in the North, the People's Army is not only the guardian of the socialist regime but also a builder of socialism. This is a glorious tradition that our army has to maintain firmly and develop constantly.

Our Party has always paid attention to the *solidarity between our army and our people and the armies and peoples of the brother countries, and the peace-loving people in the world*. Our Party has not only educated the army in genuine patriotism but also proletarian internationalism thoroughly. The units, predecessors of the army had once fought under the slogans " national liberation ", " defence of the Soviet Union ". In the Resistance War, the Viet Nam People's Volunteer Units raised to great heights the proletarian international spirit, did not shun from dangers and difficulties to fight French aggressive colonialists, shoulder to shoulder with the people of the friendly countries. Many of our comrades shed their blood for the independence, peace and closer friendship of the Indochinese peoples. Our army has devoted great attention to the strengthening and development of friendship with the people and armies of the countries in the socialist camp in the struggle for peace and socialism and against the common enemy — warmongering imperialism. Our officers and men attach great importance to the learning of the invaluable experiences of the armies of the brother countries, first of all the Soviet Army and the Chinese People's Liberation Army. The success of our army is also that of the application of Marxist-Leninist military theory, the creative application to the practical conditions of our country of the advanced experiences in building and fighting of the armies of the brother countries. Great attention was paid by our army to the strengthening of the solidarity between our people and the French people and peoples of the French colonies. It is for this reason that in fighting, our army differentiated between the French aggressive colonialists and the French and colonial toiling people who were deceived or coerced into becoming mercenary soldiers.

By differentiating between the colonial high-ranking officers and the soldiers and subalterns, and the enemy's unjust war from our just war, our army carried into effect the principle of *disintegrating the enemy*. Our troops were educated by our Party to give due consideration to propaganda work among the enemy soldiers, to enlighten them so that they could understand that they were not fighting for their own interests but as cannon-fodder to bring wealth to the colonialists. They acquainted them with our lenient policy towards prisoners of war and those who had gone over to our side of their own accord so that they would join our ranks and turn their arms against the enemy. In the course of the Resistance War, thanks to good propaganda work among enemy and puppet troops and strict implementation of our policy towards prisoners of war and those who had of their own accord passed over to our side, and thanks to the skilful co-ordination between armed struggle and political offensive, our army and people brought over to our side tens of thousands of enemy soldiers, thus throwing the enemy ranks into bewilderment and disintegration and making an important contribution to our military success.

In leading the building of the army, our Party has firmly stuck to the principle of democratic centralism. That is the organisational principle of our Party ; thereby it has taken care to build the army with a genuine inner democracy and also a very strict conscious discipline.

Completely different from all types of armies of the exploiting class, our army put into practice the *regime of internal democracy* from its inception because the internal relations between officers and men as well as the relations between the army and the people express complete unity of mind. Owing to the demand of the revolutionary work, there are in our army differences in ranks and offices, but they have not and cannot influence the relations of political equality in the army. For this reason, internal democracy should and could be carried out in the army. To practise democracy is also to apply the mass line of the Party in leading the army.

During the Resistance War, democracy was exercised in three ways and brought about good results. Political democracy: at grass-root level, democratic meetings and army congresses were held regularly so that men as well as officers had the opportunity to speak their views on fighting, work, study and living questions. In our army, not only have the officers the right to criticise the soldiers but the latter also have the right to criticise the former. Military democracy : in fighting as well as in training, democratic meetings were called whenever circumstances permitted, to expound plans, promote initiatives and together try to overcome difficulties in order to fulfil their tasks. Economic democracy : in our army, the officers and soldiers have the right to take part in the managament of the improvement of material life. Finance is made public. Thanks to the carrying out of democracy in an extensive way, we succeeded in promoting the activity and creativeness of the masses of officers and men, and concentrating their wisdom to solve the most difficult and complicated problems; also thanks to it, internal unity was strengthened and the combativeness of our army increased.

On the basis of the democratic regime, our army still has a very strict *conscious discipline*. When we speak of conscious discipline, it means that it is built up on the basis of political consciousness of the officers and men, and the most important method for maintaining discipline is education and persuasion, thus making the armymen of their own accord, respect and remind each other to observe discipline. When we speak of strict discipline, it means that everyone in the army, regardless of rank or office must observe discipline and no infringements are allowed.

Our army has always thought highly of discipline because it has been educated by the Party and knows that discipline is one of the factors that improve the combativeness of the army. As an armed collective whose task is fighting and to ensure single-mindedness and united action for its own preservation and destruction of the enemy, our army cannot abstain from having centralisation to a high degree and strict discipline. Therefore, right from its inception, absolute obedience to orders and strict observance of discipline were written down clearly in the ten pledges of honour. Thanks to that, the tasks set by the Party were fulfilled and all fighting orders thoroughly carried out in extremely hard and arduous circumstances, and in its contact with the people, our army has firmly maintained mass discipline. Nowadays, our army has entered the period of building itself into a regular and modern army, consequently demands in discipline, centralisation and unification are all the higher.

To carry out internal democracy and strengthen conscious discipline is a process of struggle against the deviations that manifest themselves in two opposite tendencies. The first tendency puts great emphasis upon discipline while disregarding democracy. In the early stage of the building of the army, a number of officers tainted with the militarist manner and habits of previous armies, advocated absolute reliance on orders and punishment in the management of the army. In the new stage of building the army, when the question of turning it into a regular army was posed and regulations issued, there came to light in a number of units the tendency to lay too much stress on centralisation and unification, with insufficient attention to the extension of democracy and the mass line, relying solely on punishments and administrative orders and overlooking education and persuasion. The second tendency was that of breaking down of discipline. During the Resistance War, this tendency was expressed in using the difficult circumstances of the guerilla war as a pretext to neglect reporting to and asking instructions from higher echelons and to ignore co-ordination in fighting. These were symptoms of undisciplined liberalism, loose carrying out of fighting orders, non-observance of battlefront discipline, infringements on mass discipline, etc... In the new stage of building the army, this is the tendency to slight centralisation and unification, wanting a free and easy life and having their own way, showing itself careless in carrying out organisation and regulations.

The two above-mentioned erroneous tendencies are both expressions of non-proletarian ideologies. The first one is the manifestation of the influence of bourgeois ideology in the management of the army. The second is the expression of lack of discipline of the peasantry and petty-bourgeoisie who made up the majority of our officers and men. Therefore, the key to a correct implementation of the democratic regime, consolidation of strict and self-conscious discipline is constantly to educate our army in proletarian ideology in order to wipe'out the remaining non-proletarian thoughts.

Democracy and discipline in the army reflect the principle of democratic centralisation of our Party. Therefore, to put into practice genuine democracy, heighten discipline, strengthen centralisation and unification, the life of the Party organisation must be consolidated. The internal democracy and iron discipline of our Party are the basis for democratic centralism and for the strict discipline of our army.

To maintain and consolidate the absolute leadership of the Party in the army, to increase political work as the sinews of our army, to intensify proletarian ideological education for officers and men, to implement the principle of internal unity, solidarity between the army and the people and international solidarity, to cause disintegration of the enemy, to put into practice the democratic regime parallel with a strict conscious discipline, are fundamental principles of the building of our army and an essential safeguard for it to maintain its people's nature, for its development and success.

3. Together with the defining of the principles of political building of the army, our Party has successfully solved the questions of organisation of the formation, equipment, supply, training, management, etc in order gradually to turn our army from a guerilla army to a regular and modern army in the particular conditions of our country.

Unlike the armies of many other countries, ours was at first only small guerilla units born in the course of the revolutionary struggle of the people of a colonial and semi-feudal country which, with bare hands, rose up to fight imperialism and its stooges. Through a long and hard struggle, our army has grown in the fighting, has won glorious victories and liberated half of the country. The small guerilla units have now grown into a large powerful people's army and is being formed into a regular modern army, when a half of the country is liberated and is building socialism. Our Party met very big difficulties in the building of the army, owing to the backward state of our economy and the need for our army to fight without cessation. Having thoroughly grasped the class viewpoint and the practical viewpoint of Marxism-Leninism, our Party has successfully solved a series of problems in building the army and has accumulated many invaluable experiences.

First of all the question of *formation* had to be solved. The army is organised in order to defeat the enemy, therefore the formation of the army must meet the demand of the realities in fighting, and be in harmony with the strategic guiding principle and the principle of fighting in each stage of the war. The organisation must be in line with our possibilities in equipment and supply, based on the national economy and in harmony with the practical conditions of the battlefields in our country.

In the early stage of the Resistance War, our army was in extremely difficult conditions, short of arms and munitions, its formation varied from one locality to another. Parallel with the gradual development from guerilla warfare to mobile warfare and with better supply and equipment, we had, from scattered units, gradually organised concentrated ones, then regiments and divisions of a regular army. In the units of the regular army, the organisation was unified step by step. The regiments and divisions were made up at first of infantrymen only. Later there were units of support and later sappers units and light artillery units, etc. To meet the mobile conditions of guerilla warfare and mobile warfare, we worked out plans of " good soldiers and reduction of organisation to its simplest form " to lighten and strengthen the command, and increase the fighting force of the unit.

In the new stage of the building of the army, to meet the requirements of modern fighting, we have, on the basis of improving and strengthening equipment, readjusted the organisation of the army, turning it from an army of infantry into an army made up of various arms. We must continue to take into consideration the infantry and concurrently strengthen the technical arms, developing them in a harmonious way, and at the same time strengthening the command at all levels with a view to increasing the combativeness of our army in the conditions of combined operations. It is also necessary, from practical training and manœuvres, to study the improvement of the formation to make it more appropriate day by day.

Being a revolutionary army under the Party's leadership, its organisation must also be imbued with the organisational principle and method of Party's leadership in the army. For this reason, we have set up, parallel with the system of command, a system of political commissars, in line with the principle that the commander and the political commissar are both heads of the unit. Corresponding with the maturity of the army and parallel with the strengthening and improvement of the staffs and logistics, due consideration has been given to the strengthening and improvement of the organs engaged in political work at all levels in order to maintain and strengthen the Party work and political work in the army.

To organise an army, the *question of equipment* must be solved because arms and equipment are the material basis of the combativeness of the army. Without arms it is of no use to speak of organising an army and of waging armed struggle. In the first stage of the building of the army, owing to our backward national economy, with almost no industry, and with the army's rear in mountain and rural areas only, the equipping of our army encountered many difficulties. The Party pointed out to the army that it had to look for its equipment on the front line, to capture the enemy weapons to arm itself and shoot at the enemy with his guns. We scored great success in implementing this principle. The great part of our regular army and guerilla units were armed with weapons captured on the battlefronts. The French Expeditionary Corps practically became carriers engaged in supplying our army with U.S.-type arms. On the other hand, our Party guided the workers in the spirit of self-reliance, and found means to manufacture a part of the arms and munitions for the army. In circumstances of extreme hardship and privation, the workers in the arms-factories raised to new heights the heroic and creative spirit of the Vietnamese working class, overcoming very great material and technical difficulties in order to turn scrap-iron into weapons for our troops to exterminate the enemy.

In these circumstances, our Party educated the army to develop the fine nature of a revolutionary army to increase the political supremacy in order to make good our weakness in equipment. Hence our army succeeded, with inferior arms, in defeating the enemy who was many times stronger in weapons. It has become an extremely fine tradition of our army — to vanquish modern weapons with an heroic spirit. However, because of our inferior weapons, in the Resistance War our army and people had to fight in extremely hard and difficult circumstances, to make great sacrifices and shed much blood. We must always realise that inferiority in arms and equipment is a big weakness that must be overcome at all costs.

At present, the building of the army has stepped into a new stage. Our army must, step by step, grow into a modern revolutionary army, able to frustrate the aggressive plots of the U.S. imperialists and their myrmidons. For this reason, improving and increasing technical equipment for the army has become a pressing demand. The replacing of the backward material and technical basis of our army by more and more modern equipment and technique is a real revolution. This technical revolution in the army is a part of the great technical revolution that is being carried on by our Party in the society of north Viet Nam. It requires great efforts in strengthening equipment, raising the organisational and managerial level as well as the ability to master and to use new techniques. The solving of the problems of equipment and technique for the army cannot be separated from the building of the material and technical basis of socialism. Nowadays, we have favourable conditions : peace has been restored and the North completely liberated. Efforts must be made to build economy and develop culture, step-by-step to carry out the industrialisation of the country in order to put an end to our economic backwardness. This is not only a great revolutionary task aimed at carrying the North to socialism but also of utmost importance to strengthen national defence and create new conditions for the improvement of the equipment and technical basis of our army.

To enable the army to master and skilfully use the weapons, raise the technical and tactical level, we must take into account the *training of the troops.* Good training is imperative in the active preparation for the fighting. The aim of training being to defeat the enemy, training must meet this requirement. The content of the training must be imbued with the strategic guiding principle and the leading ideas of our army in fighting, must be based on the enemy's practical situation and ours, and on those of the battle-fronts. Our army is still young, with a limited fighting experience. It must endeavour to learn the advanced experiences of the armies of the brother countries, first of all, the Soviet Union and China. We must thoroughly understand the practical viewpoint and proceed from the practical situation of our country in assimilating the experiences of the other countries, doing it in a critical, selective and creative way. Thus we have to combat both empiricism and dogmatism.

In the building of the army, we have, in the main, met the above-mentioned requirements. During the Resistance War, owing to constant fighting, the training of our troops could not be carried out continuously for a lengthy period but only between battles or campaigns. We actively implemented the guiding principles " To train and to learn while we fight ". After the difficult years at the beginning of the Resistance War, we succeeded in giving good training to our army. The practical viewpoint in this training deserves to be highlighted. The content of training became most practical and rich. Training was in touch with practical fighting : the troops were trained in accordance with the next day's fighting, and victory or defeat in the fighting was the best gauge for the control and assessment of the result of the training. On the basis of gradual unification of the organisation and its equipment, the content of training in the various units of the regular army was also systematised step by step. Applying in a creative way the invaluable fighting experiences of the brother armies, particularly the Chinese People's Liberation Army, we won victories in campaigns of an ever-larger scale and concurrently enriched our own fighting experiences.

At present, in peace time, we are building a regular and modern army, where training becomes a long-term central and permanent task. It is necessary to carry out regular training systematically and according to plan, proceeding from the rank and file upwards. To meet the requirements of modern war, the army must be trained to master modern technique, tactical use of arms, co-ordinated tactics and modern military science. For that, we must on the one hand, strive to learn the advanced experiences of the brother armies, and on the other, to take into good account the invaluable fighting experiences of our army. The summing up of experiences must be combined with the study of principles of modern fighting, and an appropriate content of training must proceed from the Party's military line and the enemy's practical situation and ours and of the topography.

As is said above, step-by-step modernisation of the army is virtually a technical revolution. The more strengthened are the material basis and modern technique, the more the men are required who are able to master that technique. Otherwise, modern technical equipment cannot develop its effectiveness and the army's combativeness will not be increased. This is a great responsibility in training.

In training, *training of officers* is central. The officers have been tested and tempered in actual fighting and have experience in building the army and leading the fighting. However, because they have grown up in the circumstances of guerilla war, our officers are weak in modern tactics. Therefore, while they have to ceaselessly raise their political and ideological level, consolidate their class stand and cultivate Marxist-Leninist theory, they must do their best to advance their cultural level and level of military technical science to become good military cadres of the Party, serving as the core of a modern and regular revolutionary army. This is a work of particular importance in the building of the army at the present time.

With the development and growth of the army, in the process of changing step by step from scattered to concentrated units, the necessary *rules* and *regulations* took shape. Parallel with the step by-step implementation of the relative unification of formation and training, we gradually worked out the system of supply, regulations for order in army life, reward and punishment and care of arms, etc.. Nevertheless, as our army was formerly in the process of changing from guerilla units to regular units, the demand for centralisation and unification was still at a low degree, thus systematic unified rules and regulations for the whole army were not issued. The building of the army has now entered a new stage, that of turning into a regular and modern army. A modern army is made up of many arms, and modern fighting is combined operations of various arms, carried out on a large scale and at a high tempo. Consequently, a high degree of centralisation and unification, of organisational spirit, disciplinary spirit, spirit of planning and accuracy in all the army's activities had to be carried out. The rules and regulations become a great necessity to serve as a united basis for everybody and to meet the demand of combined operations and united command.

Our army is a people's army placed under the Party's leadership, the provisions in its rules and regulations must fully express the revolutionary nature of the army, really grasp the organisational principle and method of Party's leadership in the army. These rules and regulations must come out of the practical situation of our country and of our army, and must maintain and develop its fine traditions and habits.

In recent time, the system of military service, system of service of officers and n.c. officers (including the system of grade and rank), the system of pay and that of rewards have been carried out and have brought good results. Regulations of inner order, discipline and military police have been issued and have an important effect on all aspects of unification of the whole army and in building a regular army.

The great experiences in the building of the army from the military aspect are dealt with briefly above. Practice has shown that parallel with a thorough understanding of the principles of building the army politically, if we do not correctly solve the complicated questions in the building of the military side, it would be impossible to turn a small and weak guerilla army with a scattered organisation, rudimentary weapons, low military level, and having no rules, into a powerful people's army with many arms, ever-improving technical equipment, regular training, and unified rules and regulations without attention to military matters. These are most valuable experiences. They are principles that must be adhered to in order to build our army into a powerful people's army, that is becoming a regular, modern army.

4. Parallel with the building of a strong people's army, our Party has paid great importance to the problem of building the militia and developing the reserve; at the same time, it correctly solved the relation between the army and the rear.

During the process of its formation and development, the people's armed force not only include a regular and local armies but also a big self-defence force. Immediately after the Party had set the task of preparing for an armed uprising, on the basis of the intensified political movement of the masses, there appeared the multiformed semi-armed and armed organisations, aimed at gradually shifting the masses' political struggle to the armed struggle. These were the organisational forms of self-defence units, of fighting self-defence units, then of guerilla teams in the underground armed bases in the Viet Bac mountain region. In a number of region, when the first units of the People's

Army came into being, around these units, considered as the main force, local armed units were formed ; in addition there were the immense semi-armed forces. When he ordered the creation of the Viet Nam Liberation Armed Propaganda Unit, President Ho Chi Minh paid great attention to the formation of the armed and semi-armed forces and the maintenance of the relation of solidarity and coordination between them. In the Resistance War, the more the armed struggle developed, the clearer became the differentiation between these three armed forces. The People's Army included the regular divisions and regiments, and also the local regiments, battalions or companies. Besides the regular and local armies, there were broad guerilla forces which developed everywhere throughout the country. The regular forces had the task of waging mobile warfare on a large battlefront aimed at annihilating the enemy forces. The local army had the task of fighting locally and combining its action with the regular army or with the guerilla units. The latter had the task of defending the villages, participating in production, and combining with the local and the regular army in the preparation of the battlefront as well as in the attack. The existence of the three abovementioned armed forces fully met the aspirations of the people, was instrumental in developing the army's and people's fighting force, and trained the whole people to fight the enemy. *It concretely embodied the policy of arming the whole people, and it was the form of organisation of the armed force of the people's war and the revolutionary war.*

Our Party advocated that to launch the people's war, it was necessary to have three kinds of armed forces. It attached great importance to the building and development of self-defence units and guerilla units. In our country, the militia was set up everywhere. It is thanks to the founding of people's administration everywhere in the countryside and the existence of Party branches in every place, that the militia spread far and wide, and the people rose to fight. In the enemy's rear, the guerilla units, in co-ordination with the regular army, scattered and wore out the enemy, nailed them to their bases, so that our regular army could launch mobile fighting to annihilate them. They turned the enemy rear into our front-line, and built guerilla bases as starting points for our regular army's offensive right in the heart of the enemy ; they protected the people and their property, fought the enemy and kept up production, and frustrated the enemy's schemes to use war to feed war, and of using Vietnamese to fight Vietnamese. In the free zones, the guerilla units effectively fought the enemy and kept watch on traitors ; they were effective instruments for the local administration and local Party ; at the same time, they were the shock force in production and in transport and supply. Through the process of combat and work, and having been educated and trained by the Party, the guerilla units became an inexhaustible and precious source of replenishment for the regular army, supplied the people's army with men and officers, politically well-educated and rich in fighting experience. This was a very great achievement, and at the same time a rich experience for our Party in leading the war and building the revolutionary armed forces.

The situation has now changed and the revolution has shifted to a new stage, and our People's Army is becoming a regular and modern army. If a new war breaks out, it will be a modern one. But on our side, this war will always be, in nature, a people's war ; the strengthening of national defence and the safeguarding of the Fatherland will always be the common task of our people, consequently, instead of playing a minor part, the militia will be more important ; the militia will always be a strategic force, and the guerilla war a strategic problem. As formerly, in the future, our armed forces will not only include the regular and modern army, but also the people's armed and semi-armed forces which co-ordinate with the army in military operations. At present, in peace time, north Viet Nam is advancing to socialism, the struggle between two paths, socialism or capitalism, is being waged in town and countryside. We must consolidate and intensify proletarian dictatorship ; thus the strengthening and reinforcement of the self-defence units in the countryside, cities, offices and enterprises have all the more a significance. Parallel with the building of a permanent army, a great reserve must be built, aimed at organising and educating the masses militarily, thus preparing everybody to defend the Fatherland and shatter the enemy's aggressive scheme. The base of the reserve is the self-defence units. Their tasks are:

a) To replenish the permanent army ;

b) To maintain security and protect production ;

c) To serve the front-line and carry out guerilla activities in war time.

This is the important part played by the militia and the reserve. After the restoration of peace, chiefly when the military service was experimenting, there appeared a tendency to belittle the militia, separating the militia from the reserve and considering the latter as the only force to replenish the regular army. Since this deviation was rectified, the situation has improved. The carrying out of the military service is supported by the masses, and the organisation of self-defence units and of the reserve is strongly developed.

To consolidate and develop the self-defence units, to build a strong reserve is a most important task, especially in peace time, when a substantial reduction has been made in the strength of the permanent army in order to divert manpower to economic reconstruction. To perform this task satisfactorily, it is necessary to thoroughly grasp the theory of the people's war and people's army, to stick to the class line in organisation and education, to develop the militia's fine tradition and precious experience, and to strengthen the close relation between the permanent army and the militia and the reserve. At the same time, the leadership of Party Committees in the local military organs in particular and the militia and the reserve in general must be improved.

* * *

One cannot speak of the armed struggle and the building of the revolutionary armed forces without mentioning *the problem of the rear.* This is an important problem of strategic significance and a decisive factor to the outcome of armed struggle and in the building of the armed forces.

At the beginning of World War Two, when our Party set the task of preparing for the armed insurrection, we had no armed forces and not a single inch of free land as a spring-board for our activities. Afterwards, the underground armed bases were gradually created, and the resistance bases in the rural areas of six Viet Bac provinces were founded. The experience gained in the August Revolution clearly proved the importance of the resistance bases. It showed the correct leadership of our Party in organising the resistance bases, and in founding the Viet Bac liberated zone.

This lesson was illustrated on a larger scale in the long Resistance War. The problem of resistance bases and the rear was stressed at the beginning of the Resistance War; throughout the Resistance War, the safeguarding of resistance bases and the consolidation of the rear were considered by our Party as of the utmost importance. Because they wanted to crush our leading organ and smash our Resistance, the French colonialists used every scheme to raze our resistance bases, but they suffered defeat after defeat and finally collapsed. Our armymen and people fought heroically to protect the Viet Bac resistance base — the main one in the Resistance War — and the free zones in the fourth and fifth interzones and in Nam Bo.

Due to the war situation, guerilla war developed everywhere throughout the regions occupied by the enemy. Consequently, besides these big bases, our army and people set up many others on all battlefronts in central, north and south Viet Nam, thus creating a very serious threat to the enemy and a spring-board for our army to attack them. Parallel with the fight against the enemy, in order to safeguard the resistance bases and consolidate the rear, our Party implemented positive lines of action in every aspect, did its utmost to mobilise, educate and organise the masses, to increase production, practise economy, and build local armed and semi-armed forces. Thanks to that, our resistance bases were continually strengthened, and constantly furthered their great effect on the development of the army as well as on the work of serving the frontline. Therefore, we could carry on our long Resistance War and win glorious victory in the end.

At present, north Viet Nam is entirely liberated; it is the vast rear of our army. We know that in modern warfare the rear is all the more important. Strengthening of the rear ranks first among the permanent factors which determine the victory of the war. Modern warfare requires the highest development of all the economic, political and military potentialities. Marxism-Leninism has shown that "at present, war is an overall test of the material and spiritual forces for each country". Having seen the importance of the problem of the rear, the resolution taken by the 12th Session of the Central Committee in 1957 pointed out : " We must have a plan for building and consolidating the rear in every aspect. We must enable our rear to have full material and spiritual abilities to ensure all the needs for the building of an army in peace time, as well as for the requirements of life and fighting in time of war. In every aspect of State work, in the State's general plan as well as in the plan of each branch, it is necessary to take into consideration the building and consolidation of the rear, and to combine economic and cultural needs with those of national defence and the needs in peace time with those in war. While carrying on the task of building the army, it is necessary for the army itself to pay due attention to and actively participate in the work of consolidating the rear, particularly the implementation of the economic and financial policies, and the work of production and economy. "

Proceeding from the revolutionary task in the present stage, our rear is, on a national scale, the entirely liberated north Viet Nam which is advancing to socialism. It is the revolutionary base for the whole country. Therefore, we must fully realise the importance of this rear, in order to intensify and consolidate north Viet Nam in every aspect. Parallel with the intensification and consolidation of national defence, and the building of the armed forces, we must strive to strengthen the rear in the political and economic spheres. We must actively carry out socialist transformation, strengthen the social regime and the State regime, intensify dictatorship towards the anti revolutionaries, educate the masses in patriotism and love for socialism, and raise the people's vigilance and concern in national defence, thereby ensuring the stability of the rear against all emergencies. We must do our best to build economy, develop socialist industry and agriculture in order constantly to raise the people's livelihood, at the same time to cater for the material needs of the army.

At present, peace has been restored in our country. The world situation is developing to the advantage of peace. But our country is still partitioned. American imperialism is striving to turn south Viet Nam into a new type colony and a military base. They are intervening in Laos and threatening the security of north Viet Nam. In view of this situation, it is of utmost importance to keep the correct relation between the army and the rear, between national defence and economy. On the one hand, we continue to cut down military expenditure to concentrate on economic construction ; only thus can the building of socialism, consolidation of the rear and improvement of our people's livelihood be pushed forward, and concurrently good bases created for the strengthening of national defence. On the other hand, we must do everything in our power to raise the quality of the army, develop the militia and the reserve, at the same time thoroughly realising the requirements of national defence in economic construction. If we succeed in doing so, the socialist construction in north Viet Nam will win greater victories and the North will become a more stable base for the struggle for national reunification.

∴

On the occasion of the 30th anniversary of the founding of the Party, we are happy and enthusiastic on looking back on the glorious path traversed by our Party. Our people firmly believe in and are proud of the achievements of our Party, headed by President Ho Chi Minh.

Historical experience proves that *the armed struggle has occupied an important position* in the revolutionary agitation in our country, *the people's armed forces have played an important role* in winning victories for the revolution. By taking up to armed struggle at the correct time, our people had advantageous conditions for success in the August Revolution; it is thanks to the determination to wage a long armed struggle that our people succeeded in the Resistance War.

Historical experience proves that, from its founding, our Party has held the exclusive leadership in the people's revolutionary movement, the armed struggle and the building of the revolutionary armed forces; it has led our people determinedly to fight against imperialism and feudalism. There is no party, but ours, which is capable of doing so. *It was the Party's leadership which was the fundamental guarantee of the success of our people's armed struggle.* It is only our Party, embodying the working class' determination and radical revolutionary will, which had the courage to lead our unarmed people to rise up against the

French and drive out the Japanese, wage the Resistance war with primitive weapons, and score heroic achievements. Armed with Marxist-Leninist theory full of great vigour, our Party and only our Party could work out correct political and military lines appropriate to the practical conditions of our country, to bring our people's armed struggle to success. This political line was the national people's democratic line advancing to socialism. This military line was the people's war and people's army line.

The great victory of Dien Bien Phu has gloriously ended the long period of armed struggle of our people under the leadership of our Party. At present, our people have shifted to the period of political struggle to continue the national democratic revolution in the whole country and bring north Viet Nam to socialism. Our people have a great desire for peace, our policy is to do our utmost to safeguard peace. However, the shift to the political struggle and our peace policy do not mean in any way that, from now on, in the long struggle to achieve its revolutionary task, it is no longer necessary for our Party to prepare to shatter every aggressive scheme of the enemy and to build and strengthen the armed forces. That is why, at present, in north Viet Nam, while the task of building economy and culture becomes the main work, *our Party still considers the work of consolidating national defence, strengthening the revolutionary armed forces, and building the people's army into a regular and modern army* as « one of the main tasks for the whole Party and people » (Resolution of the 12th Session of the Central Committee).

The revolutionary task of our Party and people is still very heavy. The struggle to achieve the national democratic revolution in the whole country and to bring north Viet

Nam to socialism, to win complete victory for socialism and communism in our country as well as in the world, is still a long and hard process. To strive to study the rich experiences of the armed struggle and of the building of the revolutionary armed forces, and creatively to apply them to the new historical situation in order to push forward the strengthening of national defence and buiding of the army, are tasks of practical significance on the occasion of the 30th anniversary of the founding of our glorious Party.

DIEN BIEN PHU

Dien Bien Phu was the greatest victory scored by the Viet Nam People's Army in the long war of liberation against the aggressive Franco-American imperialists. Dien Bien Phu marked an important turn in the military and political situation in Indochina. It made a decisive contribution to the great success of the Geneva Conference which restored peace in Indochina, on the basis of respect for the principles of the national sovereignty, independence, unity and territorial integrity of Viet Nam and its two friendly neighbouring countries, Cambodia and Laos.

On the anniversary of the Dien Bien Phu victory, I want to bring out in this pamphlet a number of experiences of our Party in the conduct of the war, and to recall to memory the determination of the People's Army to fight and to win, and our people's devotion in serving the front. The solidarity of our army and people in the struggle under the leadership of the Party was the decisive factor in our success. And this is the greatest lesson we have drawn from our experiences. Dien Bien Phu taught us that :

" A weak and small nation and a people's army, once resolved to stand up, to unite together and to fight for independence and peace, will have the full power to defeat all aggressive forces, even those of an imperialist power such as imperialist France aided by the United States ".

OUTLINE OF THE SITUATION OF HOSTILITIES IN WINTER 1953 — SPRING 1954

At the start of Winter 1953 the patriotic war of our people entered its eighth year.

Since the frontier campaign (1), our army had scored successive victories in many campaigns and kept the initiative on all battlefronts in north Viet Nam. After the liberation of Hoa Binh, the guerilla bases in the Red River delta were extended, and vast areas in the North-West were won back one after the other. The enemy found themselves in a daily more dangerous situation, and were driven on to the defensive. The Franco-American imperialists saw that to save the situation they had to bring in reinforcements, re-shuffle generals and map out a new plan. At that time, the war in Korea had just come to an end. The U. S. imperialists were more and more involved in plotting to protract and extend the war in Indochina. It was in these circumstances that they worked out the "Navarre plan" — a plan to continue and extend the war — which had been carefully studied and prepared in Paris and Washington.

In a word, *the "Navarre plan" was a large-scale strategic plan aimed at wiping out the greater part of our main*

---

(1) The counter-offensive in the Viet Nam-China border region in 1950.

forces within eighteen months, and occupying our whole terri-
tory, in order to turn Viet Nam permanently into a colony and
military base of the American and French imperialists.

In accordance with this plan, in the first stage, fairly
strong mobile forces would be regrouped in the Red River
delta to attack and wear out our main forces, at the same
time occupying Dien Bien Phu with a view to turning the
temporarily occupied area in the North-West into a strong
springboard.

Then, availing themselves of the rainy season, when
our main forces might be expected to be worn out and
unable to engage in any notable activity, the enemy would
rush forces to the South to occupy all our free zones and
guerilla-bases in the Fifth zone [1] and Nam Bo. [2]

Then, during Autumn Winter 1955, after the
"pacification" of the South, very strong mobile forces
would be regrouped on the battlefront of the North for
the launching of a big offensive against our rear. Starting
simultaneously from the delta and Dien Bien Phu, the
powerful mobile mass of the French army would annihilate our main forces, occupy our free zone and bring the
war to a successful end. Had this plan succeeded, our
country would have been turned into a colony of the
Franco-American imperialists, a military base from which
they could carry out new aggressive schemes.

In Autumn 1953, General Navarre launched this
machiavellian strategic plan. With the slogans "always
keep the initiative" and "always on the offensive", the

---

(1) During the war, as the French cut off all the main lines of communication
Viet Nam was divided into many zones, each embracing five or six provinces
(2) Administrative division of Viet Nam Bac Bo (Northern part) Trung Bo
(Central part) and Nam Bo (Southern part).

High Command of the French Expeditionary Corps concentrated in the Red River delta 44 mobile battalions, launched fierce mopping-up operations in its rear, attacked Ninh Binh, Nho Quan, threatened Thanh Hoa, parachuted troops on Lang Son and threatened Phu Tho. At the same time, they armed local bandits to sow confusion in the North-West. Then, on January 20, 1954, Navarre dropped parachute troops to occupy Dien Bien Phu. His plan was to reoccupy Na San, consolidate Lai Chau and extend the occupied zone in the North-West.

About November, after wiping out a part of the enemy's forces on the Ninh Binh battlefront, our army opened the Winter-Spring campaign to smash the "Navarre plan" of the American and French imperialists.

In December 1953, our troops marched on the North-West, annihilated an important part of the enemy's manpower, liberated Lai Chau and encircled Dien Bien Phu.

Also in December, the Pathet Lao forces and the Viet Nam People's Volunteers launched an offensive in Middle Laos, wiped out important enemy forces, liberated Thakhek and reached the Mekong river.

In January 1954, in the Fifth zone, our troops launched an offensive on the Western Highlands, annihilated considerable enemy manpower, liberated the town of Kontum, and came into contact with the newly liberated Bolovene Highlands, in Lower Laos.

Also in January of that year, the Pathet Lao forces and the Viet Nam People's Volunteers launched an offensive in Upper Laos, swept away important enemy forces, liberated the Nam Hu basin and threatened Luang Prabang.

Throughout this period, in the areas behind the enemy lines in north Viet Nam, in Binh Tri Thien [1], as well as in the southernmost part of Trung Bo and in Nam Bo, guerilla warfare was greatly intensified.

In the second week of March, thinking that the period of offensive of our troops was at an end, the enemy regrouped a part of his forces to resume the " Atlanta " campaign in the South of Trung Bo and occupy Quy Nhon on March 12.

On the next day, March·13, our troops *launched the big offensive against the Dien Bien Phu entrenched camp.*

Our troops fought on the Dien Bien Phu battlefield for 55 days and nights until the complete destruction of the entrenched camp on May 7, 1954.

The Winter-Spring campaign of our army ended with an historic victory.

This is in broad outline the situation of hostilities on the various battlefronts in Autumn-Winter 1953 and Spring 1954.

---

(1) The three provinces of Central Viet Nam · Quang Binh, Quang Tri and Thua Thien.

STRATEGIC DIRECTION

The strategic direction of the Dien Bien Phu campaign and of the Winter 1953-Spring 1954 campaign in general, *was a typical success of the revolutionary military line of Marxism-Leninism applied to the actual conditions of the revolutionary war in Viet Nam.*

The enemy's strategy in the " Navarre plan " was aimed at solving the great difficulties of the aggressive war, in an attempt to save their situation and win a decisive victory.

Our strategy, applied in this Winter-Spring campaign, was the strategy of a people's war and of a revolutionary army. Starting from a thorough analysis of the enemy's contradictions, and developing to the utmost the offensive spirit of an army still weak materially but particularly heroic, it aimed at concentrating our forces in the enemy's relatively exposed sectors, at annihilating their manpower and liberating a part of the territory, compelling them to scatter their forces, thus creating favourable conditions for a decisive victory.

The war unleashed by the Franco-American imperialists was an unjust war of aggression. This colonial war had no other aim than to occupy and dominate our country. The aggressive nature and object of the war forced the enemy to scatter his forces to occupy the invaded localities. The carrying out of the war was for the French Expeditionary Corps a continuous process of dispersal of forces. The enemy divisions were split into regiments, then into battalions, companies and platoons, to be stationed at thousands of points and posts on the various battlefronts of the Indochina theatre of operations. The enemy found himself face to face with a contradiction : Without scattering his forces it was impossible for him to occupy the invaded territory; in scattering his forces, he put himself in difficulties. His scattered units would fall easy prey to our troops, his mobile forces would be more and more reduced and the shortage of troops would be all the more acute. On the other hand if he concentrated his forces to move from the defensive position and cope with us with more initiative, the occupation forces would be weakened and it would be difficult for him to hold the invaded territory. Now, if the enemy gives up occupied territory, the very aim of the war of re-conquest is defeated.

Throughout the Resistance War, while the enemy's forces were more and more scattered, *our strategic line was to extend guerilla warfare everywhere.* And in each theatre of operations, we chose the positions where the enemy was relatively weak to concentrate our forces there and annihilate his manpower. As a result, the more we fought, the stronger we became ; our forces grew with every passing day. *And parallel with the process of the enemy's dispersal of forces, our people's revolutionary armed forces unceasingly intensified and extended guerilla activities, while without cease carrying on the work of concentration and building up regular units. In the fighting, in the course of the formation of our forces, we went gradually from independent companies operating separately to mobile battalions, then from battalions to regiments and divisions.* The first appearance of our divisions in the battles in the Viet Nam-China border region marked our first major victory, which drove the enemy into a disadvantageous situation.

It was after the Frontier Campaign that General de Lattre de Tassigny was dispatched to Viet Nam to save the situation. Tassigny had seen the problem. He was aware of the too great dispersal of French forces, and of the danger arising from our guerilla warfare. So he energetically regrouped his forces and launched extremely fierce and barbarous mopping-up operations to " pacify" the areas behind the enemy's lines in the Red River delta. But he found himself very soon face to face with the same insoluble contradiction. By concentrating his forces he found it impossible to extend occupied territory. Tassigny had, in the end, to resign himself to scattering his forces to launch the famous offensive on Hoa Binh. The results were not long in coming. While his crack troops suffered very heavy losses at Hoa Binh, our guerilla bases in the delta were restored and widened very considerably.

In 1953, when the " Navarre plan " was being worked out, the French imperialists also found themselves faced with the same dilemma : lack of forces to win back the initiative, to attack and annihilate our main forces. They set themselves the task of building up their fighting forces again at all costs, and, in fact, they did concentrate big forces in the Red River delta. With these forces, they hoped to wear out our main forces, compel us to scatter our army between the delta and the mountainous regions, with a view to gradually carrying out their plan and preparing for a big decisive offensive.

Faced with this situation, our Party's Central Comittee made a thorough and clear-sighted analysis of the enemy's designs and of the characteristics of the theatre of operations. *The thorough understanding of the contradictions and general laws of the aggressive war enabled us to detect the enemy's great weakness arising from the concentration of his forces. Always convinced that the essential thing was to destroy the enemy's manpower, the Central Committee worked out its plan of action on the basis of scientific analysis: to concentrate our forces to move to the offensive against important strategic points where the enemy's forces were relatively weak in order to wipe out a part of his manpower, at the same time compelling him to scatter his forces to cope with us at vital points which he had to defend at all costs. Our strategic directives were: dynamism, initiative, mobility and rapidity of decision in face of new situations.*

The Central Committee's strategic direction proved itself correct and clear-sighted: while the enemy was concentrating big forces in the delta to threaten our free zone, instead of leaving our main forces in the delta or scattering our forces in the free zone to defend it by a defensive action, we regrouped our forces and boldly attacked in the direction of the North-West. Indeed, our divisions marched on the North-West with an irresistible impetus, swept away thousands of local bandits at Son La and Thuan Chau, liberated Lai Chau, cutting to pieces the greater part of the enemy's column which fled from Lai Chau. Simultaneously, we encircled Dien Bien Phu, thus compelling the enemy to carry out in haste a movement of forces to reinforce Dien Bien Phu in order to save it from being wiped out. Besides the Red River delta, Dien Bien Phu became a second point of concentration of enemy forces.

Concurrently with our offensive in the North-West, the Laos-Viet Nam joint forces launched a second offensive in an important direction where the enemy was relatively exposed, the Middle Laos front.

Several enemy mobile units were annihilated and the town of Thakhek was liberated. The joint forces pushed on in the direction of Seno, an important enemy air base in Savannakhet. The enemy had to rush forces in haste from the Red River delta and from all other battlefields to reinforce Seno, thus turning it into a third point of concentration of his forces.

Early in 1954, while the enemy was feverishly making preparations for his offensive against our free territory in the Fifth zone, our plan was to leave only a small part of our forces to protect our rear and to concentrate big forces to attack on the Western Highlands, which was an important strategic position where the enemy was relatively exposed. Our advance to the Western Highlands was accompanied by resounding victories: important enemy units were wiped out, the town and whole province of Kontum were liberated. Our troops made a raid on Pleiku, compelling the enemy to dispatch more troops there in reinforcement, turning Pleiku and various bases on the Western Highlands into a fourth point of concentration of French forces.

During the same period, to create a diversion in order to secure conditions for our troops to step up preparations at Dien Bien Phu, the Laos-Viet Nam joint forces had, from Dien Bien Phu, launched an offensive in Upper Laos. Several enemy units were wiped out and the vast Nam Hu basin was liberated. The enemy was compelled to rush more forces to Luang Prabang, which became the fifth point of concentration of French forces.

In the first phase of the Winter-Spring campaign, after three months' activity by our army, the enemy had suffered great losses on all battlefields. Many vast areas of strategic importance had been liberated and the Navarre plan of regroupment of forces was foiled. The enemy, who had made great efforts to regroup fairly strong mobile forces on a single battlefield — the Red River delta — was compelled to change his plan by concentrating his forces on a smaller scale at many different points. In other words, the Navarre plan of active regroupment of forces had in fact been turned into a forced dispersal of these same forces. The much-vaunted " Navarre mobile corps " in the delta had been reduced from 44 to 20 battalions. It was the beginning of the end of the "Navarre plan ".

For us, the first phase of the Winter-Spring campaign was a series of offensives launched simultaneously on various important sectors where the enemy was relatively exposed, in which we annihilated part of the enemy's forces and liberated occupied areas, at the same time compelling the enemy to scatter his forces in many directions. We continually kept the initiative of the operations and drove the enemy on to the defensive. Also in this period, on the main battlefront, we pinned down the enemy at Dien Bien Phu, thus creating favourable conditions for our troops on other battlefields. In the national theatre of operations, there was large-scale co-ordination between the main battlefields and the theatres of operation in the enemy's rear. In each theatre, there was also close co-ordination between the main battlefield and the fronts in the enemy's rear. On the Indochinese battlefront, Dien Bien Phu became the strongest base of regroupment of the enemy forces and therefore the most important battlefield. As Dien Bien Phu had been encircled for a long time, there were new favourable conditions for the great intensification of guerilla activities and the winning of major successes in the Red River delta, in the southern part of Trung Bo as well as in Nam Bo. The enemy lacked the forces to launch mopping-up operations on any considerable scale. During this time, our free zones were no longer threatened. Moreover, our compatriots in the free zones could go to work even in the daytime without being molested by enemy aircraft.

It was also in the course of the first phase of the Winter-Spring campaign that we completed our preparations for the assault on Dien Bien Phu. During this period, the dispositions of the fortified entrenched camp had also undergone great changes. On the one hand, the enemy's forces had been increased and their defence strengthened ; on the other hand, after the successive liberation of Lai Chau, Phong Saly and the Nam Hu river valley, Dien Bien Phu was completely isolated, some hundreds of kilometres from its nearest supply bases, Hanoi and the Plain of Jars.

From March 13, 1954, there began the second period of the Winter-Spring campaign. We launched the big offensive on the Dien Bien Phu fortified entrenched camp. This was a new step in the progress of the hostilities. Sticking firmly to our strategic principles — dynamism, initiative, mobility and rapidity of decision in face of new situations — and having the conditions for victory well in hand, we directed our main attack on the most powerful entrenched camp of the enemy. The task of our regular forces on the main battlefield was no longer to encircle and immobilise the enemy in their barracks, but to go over to the attack and to concentrate forces to annihilate the Dien Bien Phu fortified entrenched camp. The task of the other battle-fronts in the

North, Centre and South of Viet Nam was to intensify activities continuously in co-ordination with Dien Bien Phu, in order to annihilate more enemy manpower, scatter and pin down enemy forces, hampering the enemy in his efforts to reinforce Dien Bien Phu. On the Dien Bien Phu battlefield, our combatants fought with remarkable heroism and stubbornness. On all the co-ordinated battlefronts our troops did their utmost to overcome very great difficulties. They re-organised their force while fighting, and carried out the order of co-ordination with admirable determination and heroism.

Such was the essence of the strategic direction of the Dien Bien Phu campaign and of the Winter-Spring campaign as a whole. This direction drew its inspiration from the principles of dynamism, initiative, mobility and rapidity of decision in face of new situations. Its main object was the destruction of enemy manpower. It took full advantage of the contradictions in which the enemy was involved and developed to the utmost the spirit of active offensive of the revolutionary army. This correct, clear-sighted and bold strategy enabled us to deprive the enemy of all possibility of retrieving the initiative, and to create favourable conditions for us to fight a decisive battle on a battlefield chosen and prepared for by us. *This strategic direction ensured the success of the whole Winter - Spring campaign which was crowned by the great victory of Dien Bien Phu.*

DIRECTION OF OPERATIONS AT
DIEN BIEN PHU

We have expounded the essence of the strategic direction of the 1953-1954 Winter-Spring campaign. The spirit and guiding principles of this strategic direction posed two problems to be solved for the direction of operations on the Dien Bien Phu battlefield:

1. — To attack or not to attack Dien Bien Phu ?

2. — If we attack, how should we go about it ?

The parachuting of enemy troops into Dien Bien Phu was not necessarily to be followed by an attack on the fortified camp. As Dien Bien Phu was a very strongly fortified entrenched camp of the enemy we could not decide to attack it without first weighing the pros and cons very carefully. The fortified entrenched camp was a new form of defence of the enemy developed in face of the growth in the strength and size of our army. At Hoa Binh and at Na San, the enemy had already entrenched his forces in fortified camps. In the Winter-Spring campaign new fortified entrenched camps appeared not only at Dien Bien Phu but also at Seno, Muong Sai and Luang Prabang in the Laotian theatre of operations, and at Pleiku, on the Western Highlands front.

With the enemy's new form of defence, should we attack the fortified entrenched camp or should we not ?

While our forces were still obviously weaker than the enemy's we always stuck to the principle of concentration of forces to attack the points where the enemy was relatively weak to annihilate his manpower. *Our position was, time and again, to pin down the enemy's main forces in the fortified camps, while choosing more favourable directions for our attack.* In Spring 1952, when the enemy erected the fortified camps at Hoa Binh, we struck hard and scored many victories along the Da river and in the enemy's rear in north Viet Nam. In Spring 1953, when the enemy fortified Na San, we did not attack his position but intensified our activities in the delta and launched an offensive in the West. During the last months of 1953 and at the beginning of 1954, when the enemy set up fortified camps in various places, our troops launched many successful offensives on sectors where the enemy was relatively weak, and at the same time stepped up guerilla warfare behind the enemy's lines.

These tactics of attacking positions other than the fortified entrenched camps had recorded many successes. But these were not the only tactics. We could also *directly attack the fortified entrenched camp to annihilate the enemy's manpower in the heart of his new form of defence.* Only when we had wiped out the fortified entrenched camp, could we open up a new situation, paving the way for new victories for our army and people.

That was why, on the Dien Bien Phu battlefield, the problem of whether to attack or not had been posed, especially as Dien Bien Phu was the enemy's strongest fortified entrenched camp in the whole Indochina war theatre, while our troops had, up to that time, attacked only fortresses defended by one or two companies, or one battalion at most.

Dien Bien Phu being the keystone of the Navarre plan, we considered that it should be wiped out if the Franco-American imperialist plot of protracting and expanding the war was to be smashed. However, the importance of Dien Bien Phu could not be regarded as a decisive factor in our decision to attack it. In the relation of forces at that time could we destroy the fortified entrenched camp of Dien Bien Phu ? Could we be certain of victory in attacking it ? Our decision had to depend on this consideration alone.

Dien Bien Phu was a very strongly fortified entrenched camp. But on the other hand, it was set up in a mountainous region, on ground which was advantageous to us, and decidedly disadvantageous to the enemy. Dien Bien Phu was, moreover, a completely isolated position, far away from all the enemy's bases. The only means of suppling Dien Bien Phu way by air. These circumstances could easily deprive the enemy of all initiative and force him on to the defensive if attacked.

On our side, we had picked units of the regular army which we could concentrate to achieve supremacy in power. We could overcome all difficulties in solving the necessary tactical problems, we had, in addition, an immense rear, and the problem of supplying the front with food and ammunition, though very difficult, was not insoluble. Thus we had conditions for retaining the initiative in the operations.

It was on the basis of this analysis of the enemy's and our own strong and weak points that we solved the question as to whether we should attack Dien Bien Phu or not. *We decided to wipe out at all costs the whole enemy force at*

Dien Bien Phu, after having created favourable conditions for this battle by launching numerous offensives on various battlefields and by intensifying preparations on the Dien Bien Phu battlefield. This important decision was a new proof of the dynamism, initiative, mobility and rapidity of decision in face of new situations displayed in the conduct of the war by the Party's Central Committee. Our plan foresaw the launching of many offensives on the points where the enemy was relatively weak, availing ourselves of all opportunities to wipe out enemy's manpower in mobile warfare. But whenever it was possible and success was certain, we were resolved not to let slip an opportunity to launch powerful attacks on strong points to annihilate the more concentrated enemy forces. Our decision to make the assault on the Dien Bien Phu fortified camp clearly marked a new step forward in the development of the Winter-Spring campaign, in the annals of our army's battles and in the history of our people's resistance war.

We had pledged to wipe out the whole enemy force at Dien Bien Phu but we still had to solve this problem : How should we do it ? *Strike swiftly and win swiftly, or strike surely and advance surely ! This was the problem of the direction of operations in the campaign.*

In the early stage, when we began the encirclement of Dien Bien Phu, and the enemy, having been newly parachuted into the area, had not yet had time to complete his fortifications and increase his forces, the question of striking swiftly and winning swiftly had been posed. By concentrating superior forces, we could push simultaneously from many directions deep into enemy positions, cut the fortified entrenched camp into many separate parts, then swiftly annihilate the entire enemy manpower. There were many obvious advantages if we could strike swiftly to win swiftly : by launching a big offensive with fresh troops, we could shorten the duration of the campaign and avoid the wear and fatigue of a long operation. As the campaign would not last long, the supplying of the battlefront could be ensured without difficulty. However, on further examining the question, we saw that these tactics had a very great, a basic disadvantage : our troops lacked experience in attacking fortified entrenched camps. If we wanted to win swiftly, success could not be ensured. For that reason, in the process of making preparations, we continued to follow the enemy's situation and checked and re-checked our potentialities again. And we came to the conclusion that we could not secure success if we struck swiftly. In consequence, *we resolutely chose the other tactic : to strike surely and advance surely.* In taking this correct decision, *we stricly followed this fundamental principle of the conduct of a revolutionary war : strike to win, strike only when success is certain ; if it is not, then don't strike.*

In the Dien Bien Phu campaign, the adoption of these tactics demanded of us firmness and a spirit of resolution. Since we wanted to strike surely and advance surely, preparations would take a longer time and the campaign would drag out. And the longer the campaign went on the more, new and greater difficulties would crop up. Difficulties in supply would increase enormously. The danger increased of our troops being worn out while the enemy consolidated defences and lined up his forces. Above all, the longer the campaign lasted, the nearer came the rainy season with all its disastrous consequences for operations carried out on the mountains and in forests. As a result, not everybody was immediately convinced of the correctness of these tactics. We patiently educated our men, pointed out that there were real difficulties, but that our task was to overcome them to create good conditions for the great victory we sought.

It was from these guiding principles that we developed our plan of progressive attack, in which the Dien Bien Phu campaign was regarded not as *a large-scale attack on fortresses carried out over a short period, but as a large-scale campaign carried out over a fairly long period, through a series of successive attacks on fortified positions until the enemy was destroyed.* In the campaign as a whole we already had numerical superiority over the enemy. But in each attack or each wave of attacks, we had the possibility of achieving absolute supremacy and ensuring the success of each operation and consequently total victory in the campaign. Such a plan was in full keeping with the tactical and technical level of our troops, creating conditions for them to accumulate experience in fighting and to ensure the annihilation of the enemy at Dien Bien Phu.

We strictly followed these guiding principles throughout the campaign. We encircled the enemy and carried out our preparations thoroughly over a period of three months. Then, after opening the offensive, our troops fought relentlessly for 55 days and nights. Careful preparation and relentless fighting led our Dien Bien Phu campaign to resounding victory.

SOME QUESTIONS OF TACTICS

Dien Bien Phu was a fortified entrenched camp defended by fairly strong forces: 17 battalions of infantry, three battalions of artillery, without counting engineers and tank units, air and transport units, etc., most of them picked elements of the French Expeditionary Corps in Indochina. The fortified camp was made up of 49 strong-posts, organised into fortified resistance centres and grouped into three sectors capable of supporting each other. In the middle of the central sector, which was effectively guarded by the resistance centres on the hill-tops in the East, were mobile forces, artillery positions and tank units, as well as the enemy headquarters. The airfield of Dien Bien Phu was near here. This whole vast defence system lay within strong underground fortifications and trenches.

The French and American military authorities believed that the fortified entrenched camp of Dien Bien Phu was impregnable. They were certain that an offensive against Dien Bien Phu would be suicidal, that failure was inevitable. Therefore, during the first weeks of the campaign, the French High Command firmly believed that there was little possibility of an offensive against Dien Bien Phu by our army. Until the last minute, the offensive launched by our men was unexpected by the enemy.

General Navarre had over-estimated the Dien Bien Phu defences. He believed that we would be unable to crush even one centre of resistance. Because, unlike the simple strong-posts at Na San or Hoa Binh, these were centres of resistance forming a much more complex and strongly fortified defence system.

The destruction of the fortified entrenched camp as a whole was, to Navarre's mind, still less feasible. In his opinion, his artillery and air forces were powerful enough to wipe out all forces coming from outside before these could be deployed in the valley and approach the fortifications. He was not in the least worried about our artillery which he thought weak and not transportable to the approaches of Dien Bien Phu. Nor was he anxious about his own supplies, because both airfields, surrounded by the defence sectors, could not be in danger. Never did it enter his head that the whole fortified camp could be annihilated by our troops.

The enemy's estimates were obviously wishful thinking but they were not totally without foundation. In fact, the Dien Bien Phu fortified entrenched camp had many strong points which had given our army new problems of tactics to solve before we could annihilate the enemy.

The fortified entrenched camp was a defence system manned by big forces. The centres of resistance, which were closely connected to one another, were effectively supported by artillery, tank units and aircraft, and could easily be reinforced by mobile forces. This was a strong point for the enemy and for us, a difficulty. *We overcame this difficulty by applying the tactics of progressive attack,* by regrouping our forces to have great local superiority, by striving to neutralise as much as possible the enemy artillery fire and mobile forces, bringing everything into play to wipe out the centres of resistance one by one, or a group of centres at

173

one time in a wave of attacks. By concentrating forces to achieve absolute superiority at one point, we were certain to crush the enemy, especially in the first days of the campaign, when we attacked the enemy outposts.

The fortified entrenched camp had quite powerful artillery fire, tank and air forces. This was another strong point of the enemy, a very great difficulty of ours, especially since we had only very limited artillery fire and no mechanised or air forces. *We overcame this difficulty by digging a whole network of trenches that encircled and strangled the entrenched camp,* thus creating conditions for our men to deploy and move under enemy fire. Our fighters dug hundreds of kilometres of trenches These wonderful trenches enabled our forces to deploy and move in open country under the rain of enemy napalm bombs and artillery shells. But to reduce the effect of enemy fire was not enough, *we still had to strengthen our own firepower.* Our troops cut through mountains and hacked away jungles to build roads and haul our artillery pieces to the approaches of Dien Bien Phu. Where roads could not be built, artillery pieces were moved by nothing but the sweat and muscle of our soldiers. Our artillery was set up in strongly fortified firing positions, to the great surprise of the enemy. Our light artillery played a great part in the Dien Bien Phu battle.

While neutralising the enemy's strong points, we had to make the most of his weak points. His greatest weakness *lay in his supply,* which depended entirely on his air forces. Our tactics were from the very beginning to use our artillery-fire to destroy the air-strips, and our anti-aircraft guns to cope with the activities of enemy planes. Later, with the development of the waves of attacks, everything was brought into play to hinder enemy supply and gradually stop it altogether.

These are a few of the problems of tactics we solved in the Dien Bien Phu campaign. They were solved on the basis of our analysis of the enemy's strong and weak points, combining technique with the heroism and hard-working and fighting spirit of a People's Army.

To sum up, our plan of operations based upon these tactical considerations consisted in setting up a whole system of lines of attack and encirclement, permitting our forces to launch successive attacks to annihilate the enemy. This network of innumerable trenches with firing positions and command posts encircled and strangled the enemy. It was progressively extended with our victories. From the surrounding mountains and forests, it moved down into the valley. Each enemy position, once wiped out, was immediately turned into our own. As we encircled the enemy fortified entrenched camp, a real fortified camp of our own, very mobile, gradually took shape, and kept closing in, while the enemy camp was constantly narrowed down.

In the first phase of the campaign, from our newly-built network of attack and encirclement positions, we annihilated the Him Lam and Doc Lap centres of resistance, and the whole Northern sector. The enemy made desperate efforts to destroy our firing positions. Their planes poured napalm bombs on the mountains around Dien Bien Phu. Their artillery concentrated powerful fire on our firing positions. But we held on.

In the second phase, the " axis " communication trenches, with their innumerable ramifications, starting from our bases, extended down into the valley and isolated the Central sector from the Southern sector. The fierce and successful assault on the Eastern hill-tops enabled our belt of artillery fire to close in. From the captured positions, our guns of all calibres could exert pressure on the enemy. The air-strips were completely controlled by our fire.

The enemy became increasingly active, bringing reinforcements for his mobile forces, launching counter-attacks and furiously bombing our lines in an attempt to save the situation. It was a desperate positional battle. Many hilltops were captured and recaptured many times. Some were occupied half by our troops and half by the enemy. Our tactics were to encroach, harass and wrest every inch of ground from the enemy, destroy his air-strips and narrow down his free air-space.

The third phase was that of general offensive. The enemy had been driven in to an area about 1.5 to 2 kilometres square. His forces had suffered heavy losses. Once hill A-1 had been completely occupied by our troops, all hope of continued resistance vanished and the enemy's morale sank extremely low. On March 7, our troops launched an offensive from all directions, occupied the enemy headquarters and captured the whole enemy staff. That night, the Southern sector was also wiped out.

The Dien Bien Phu campaign ended in a great victory.

OUR ARMY'S DETERMINATION TO FIGHT AND TO WIN

The great task assigned to the whole army and people by the Party's Central Committee and the Government was: *to concentrate forces, to be thoroughly imbued with determination, "to actively develop the spirit of heroic fighting and endurance to bring the campaign to complete victory".* For the Dien Bien Phu campaign, as had been pointed out by President Ho Chi Minh and the Political Bureau of the Central Committee of the Viet Nam Lao Dong Party, was an historic campaign of exceptional importance to the military and political situation in our country and to the full growth of our army, as well as to the struggle for the defence of peace in South-East Asia.

Our troops fought to carry out this great task with unshakable determination. Our combatants' will to fight and to defeat the enemy was one of the decisive factors which brought the Dien Bien Phu campaign and the Winter-Spring campaign in general such brilliant victories on all battlefronts.

Throughout the history of the armed struggle of our people, never had our army been entrusted with so great and heavy a task as in Winter 1953-Spring 1954. The enemy to be annihilated was rather a strong one. Our forces thrown into the battle were very large. The theatre of operations was extensive and the operations lasted half a year. On the Dien Bien Phu battlefield, as on all other co-ordinated battlefields, our combatants, with a spirit of heroism and endurance, surmounted countless difficulties and overcame many great obstacles to annihilate the enemy and fulfil their task. This heroism and endurance were tempered and enhanced by the long years of Resistance. Particularly in Winter 1953-Spring 1954, the revolutionary enthusiasm of our combatants increased greatly after their study of the policy for the mobilization of the masses for land reform. Here, stress should be laid on the considerable contribution made by the land reform policy to the victories of the Winter-Spring campaign, particularly on the Dien Bien Phu battlefield.

On the Dien Bien Phu battlefront, in the period of preparation, our armymen opened up the supply line from Tuan Giao to Dien Bien Phu ; built through mountains and forests roads practicable for trucks to move artillery pieces into position ; built artillery emplacements ; dug trenches from the mountains to the valley ; changed the terrain; overcame enormous obstacles, and in all ways created favourable conditions for the annihilation of the enemy. Neither difficulties, fatigue nor enemy bombing and artillery fire could shake the iron will of our men.

From the first shot touching off the offensive against Dien Bien Phu, and throughout the battle, our combatants fought with extraordinary heroism. Under the deluge of bombs from the enemy air force, and under the enemy's cross-fire, our fighters valiantly stormed and captured Him Lam and Doc Lap hills, put the enemy troops entrenched on the Eastern hills out of action, expanded our bases, cut off the airfields, repulsed counter-attacks and kept tightening our encirclement. During all this time, the enemy's napalm-bombs burned down the undergrowth on the hills surrounding Dien Bien Phu, and enemy bombs and shells ploughed deep into the fields in our zones of operations. But our combatants kept moving forward to carry out their tasks. One fell, but many others rushed forward like a sweeping rising tide that no force on earth could hold back. *We witnessed a phenomenon of collective heroism in which the most admirable deeds were performed by* To Vinh Dien, *who threw himself under the wheel of an artillery piece to prevent it from slipping back;* Phan Dinh Giot, *who silenced an enemy gun nest with his own body; the shock troops who planted the banner of "Determination to Fight and to Win" on Him Lam hill, and the shock troops who captured the enemy headquarters.*

The spirit of heroism and endurance of our fighters on co-ordinated battlefields should also be mentioned. On the Western Highlands, great successes were scored at Kontum and An Khe. In the Red River delta, our troops destroyed 78 planes on Cat Bi and Gia Lam airfields, wiped out several enemy fortified positions and cut off road No. 5, the enemy's main supply line. In south Viet Nam, more than 1,000 enemy posts were annihilated or evacuated, many stocks of bombs destroyed and ships sunk. On the battlefields of our two neighbouring countries, our people's volunteers, together with the army and the people of these friendly countries, wiped out the invaders and scored many great victories.

Never had our army fought with such endurance for so long a time as in Winter 1953-Spring 1954. There were units which marched and pursued the enemy for more than 3,000 kilometres. There were others which moved secretly for more than 1,000 kilometres on the Truong Son * mountain range to take part in fighting on a far-off battlefield. The units on Dien Bien Phu battlefield moved from the delta to the mountains, and at once set passionately to work, at the same time fighting to protect their preparatory labour. Then came the battle, and our troops lived and fought for two months in trenches after having spent three months of hardship in the jungle. While the battle was going on, certain units rushed to places two or three hundred kilometres away to launch surprise attacks on the enemy, then came back to take part in the annihilation of the enemy at Dien Bien Phu. The spirit of co-operation between the various units and various arms was enhanced during the battle, and there was close co-ordination between the various battlefields.

Our combatants' *determination to fight and to win as described above came from the revolutionary nature of our army and the painstaking education of the Party. It had been enhanced in battle and in the ideological re-moulding classes.* This does not mean that, even when the Dien Bien Phu battle was at its height, negative factors never appeared. *To maintain and develop this determination to fight and to win was a whole process of unremitting and patient political and ideological education and struggle,* tireless and patient efforts in political work on the front line. This was a great achievement of the Party's organizations and branches and of its cadres. After a series of resounding victories, we found in our ranks signs of under-estimation of the enemy. By criticism, we rectified this state of mind in good time. In the long period of preparation, particularly

---

* Range of mountains running from the North to the South of Central Viet Nam, along the Viet Nam-Laos border.

after the second phase of the campaign, when attack and defence were equally fierce, negative rightist thoughts cropped up again to the detriment of the carrying out of the task. In accordance with the instructions of the Political Bureau, we opened in the heart of the battlefield an intensive and extensive struggle against rightist passivity, and for the heightening of revolutionary enthusiasm and the spirit of strict discipline, with a view to ensuring the total victory of the campaign. This ideological struggle was very successful. This was one of the greatest achievements in political work in our army's history. It led the Dien Bien Phu campaign to complete victory.

The determination to fight and to win of our army on the Dien Bien Phu and other co-ordinated battlefields was a distinctly marked manifestation of the boundless loyalty of our People's Army to the revolutionary struggle of the people and the Party. It was a collective manifestation of proletarian ideology, of the class-stand of the officers and men and Party members in the army. It maintained the Viet Nam People's Army tradition of heroic fighting, endurance and determination in the fulfilment of its duty. It made of the soldier of the People's Army an iron fighter. Dien Bien Phu will forever symbolize the traditions of fighting and winning victory of our army and people. Our military banner is the banner of *" Determination to Win "*.

PEOPLE'S DEVOTION
TO SERVING THE FRONT

The Party's Central Committee and the Government decided that the whole people and Party should concentrate all their forces for the service of the front, in order to ensure the victory of the Dien Bien Phu campaign. During this campaign, and generally speaking, during the whole Winter-Spring campaign, our whole people — workers, peasants, youth, intellectuals — every Vietnamese patriot, answered the appeal for national liberation and did his utmost to achieve the slogan *"All for the front, all for victory"* with an ardent and unprecedented enthusiasm, at the cost of superhuman efforts.

Throughout the long years of the Resistance War, our people never made so great a contribution as in the Winter 1953-Spring 1954 campaign, in supplying the army for the fight against the enemy. On the main Dien Bien Phu front, our people had to ensure the supply of food and munition to a big army, operating 500 to 700 kilometres from the rear, and in very difficult conditions. The roads were bad, the means of transport insufficient and the supply lines relentlessly attacked by the enemy. There was, in addition, the menace of heavy rains that could create more obstacles than bombing.

On the Dien Bien Phu front, the supply of food and munitions was a factor as important as the problem of tactics; logistics constantly posed problems as urgent as those posed by the armed struggle. These were precisely the difficulties that the enemy thought insuperable for us. The imperialists and traitors could never appreciate the strength of a nation, of a people. This strength is immense. It can overcome any difficulty, defeat any enemy.

The Vietnamese people, under the direct leadership of the committees of supply for the front, gave proof of great heroism and endurance in serving the front.

Truck convoys valiantly crossed streams, mountains and forests; drivers spent scores of sleepless nights, in defiance of difficulties and dangers, to bring food and ammunition to the front, to permit the army to annihilate the enemy.

Thousands of bicycles from the towns also carried food and munitions to the front.

Hundreds of sampans of all sizes, hundreds of thousands of bamboo-rafts crossed rapids and cascades to supply the front.

Convoys of pack-horses from the Meo highlands or the provinces headed for the front.

Day and night, hundreds of thousands of porters and young volunteers crossed passes and forded rivers in spite of enemy planes and delayed-action bombs.

Near the firing line, supply operations had to be carried out uninterruptedly and in the shortest possible time. Cooking, medical work, transport, etc., was carried on right in the trenches, under enemy bombing and cross-fire.

Such was the situation at Dien Bien Phu, but on the co-ordinated fronts, big armed forces were also active, especially on the Western Highlands and in other remote theatres of operation. On these fronts, as at Dien Bien Phu, our people fulfilled their tasks. They admirably solved the problems of supply to enable the army to defeat the enemy, always to win new victories.

Never had so large a number of Vietnamese gone to the front. Never had so many young Vietnamese travelled so far and become acquainted with so many distant regions of their country. From the plains to the mountains, on roads and paths, on rivers and streams, everywhere, there was the same animation: the rear sent its men and wealth to the front in order to annihilate the enemy and, together with the army, to liberate the country.

The rear brought to the fighter at the front its will to annihilate the enemy, its strong unity in the resistance and the revolutionary enthusiasm of the land reform. Each day, thousands of letters and telegrams from all over the country came to the Dien Bien Phu front. Never had Viet Nam been so anxious about her fighting sons, never had the relations between the rear and the front been so intimate as in this Winter Spring campaign.

Indeed, a strong rear is always the decisive factor for victory in a revolutionary war. In the Dien Bien Phu campaign and, generally speaking, in the whole Winter-Spring campaign, our people made a worthy contribution to the victory of the nation.

We cannot forget the sympathy and hearty support of the brother peoples, of the progressive peoples all over the world, including the French people. Every day, from all corners of the earth, from the Soviet Union, China, North Korea and the German Democratic Republic,

Algeria, India, Burma, Indonesia, and other countries news reached the front through broadcasts, bringing the expression of the boundless support of progressive mankind for the just struggle of the Vietnamese people and army. This was a very great encouragement for the combatants of the Viet Nam People's Army at Dien Bien Phu, as on all other fronts.

THE WAR OF LIBERATION OF OUR PEOPLE WAS ONE LONG AND GREAT DIEN BIEN PHU BATTLE

The victory of Dien Bien Phu and, generally speaking, the Winter 1953-Spring 1954 victories were the greatest victories won by our army and people in their long war of liberation against aggressive imperialism.

At Dien Bien Phu, our army annihilated the enemy's strongest fortified camp in Indo-China, and wiped out 16,000 of his crack troops. During this Winter-Spring campaign, for all the fronts operating in co-ordination with Dien Bien Phu, the total losses of the enemy amounted to 110,000 men.

The "Navarre plan" was smashed to pieces. The French and American imperialists failed in their attempt to prolong and extend the war in Indo-China. The Dien Bien Phu victory had very great influence. Thanks to it, and to the success scored on the other co-ordinated fronts, we liberated the capital Hanoi and also the North of Viet Nam. Thanks to it, we achieved brilliant success at the Geneva Conference, and peace was restored in Indo-China.

With the "Navarre plan", the French and American imperialists wanted to launch a decisive battle. In fact, the battle of Dien Bien Phu was decisive. Dien Bien Phu was a great victory for our army and people. Dien Bien Phu decided the humiliating defeat of the aggressive imperialists.

Dien Bien Phu was a battle in which our people and their army coped with the expeditionary corps of the French imperialists, backed by the U.S. warmongers. We won the war and the aggressive imperialists were the losers. Dien Bien Phu will forever symbolize the indomitable spirit of our people who opposed to the powerful army of an imperialist country, the unity and heroism of a weak nation and of a people's army still in its early days. This heroic spirit was the spirit of our people and army throughout the long resistance. Thus, we can assert that each of our struggles, however big or small, was imbued with "the spirit of Dien Bien Phu", that the war of liberation of our people was one long and great Dien Bien Phu battle.

We were victorious at Dien Bien Phu. Our national war ended with a great victory which showed the very clear-sighted and heroic leadership of our Party. This was a great victory of Marxism-Leninism in the liberation war of a small and heroic nation. Our people could say with pride : under the leadership of our Party headed by President Ho Chi Minh we established a great historic truth : *a colonized and weak people once it has risen up and is united in the struggle and determined to fight for its independence and peace, has the full power to defeat the strong aggressive army of an imperialist country.*

Thus, Dien Bien Phu was a victory not only for our people, but also for all weak peoples who are struggling to throw off the yoke of the colonialists and imperialists. That is the great significance of the Dien Bien Phu victory.

Therefore, its anniversary is a day for rejoicing for our whole people and also a day of great joy for the brother peoples, for the peoples who have just won back their independence, and for those who are fighting for their liberation.

Dien Bien Phu is written down forever in the annals of the struggle for national liberation of our people and of oppressed peoples all over the world. History will record it as one of the crucial events in the great movement of Asian, African and Latin American peoples who are rising up to liberate themselves and to be masters of their own destiny.

Solidarity in the struggle under the leadership of our Party led our people to the Dien Bien Phu victory. It will surely lead us to new and greater victories in the building of north Viet Nam on the way to socialism and in the struggle for national reunification by peaceful means.

APPENDIX

I — MILITARY SITUATION IN
SUMMER 1953

The winter of 1940 marked a new change in the military situation in Viet Nam. After their great victory in the Border campaign, our forces undertook a series of important campaigns : the Midland campaign, the road No. 18 campaign and the Ha Nam - Nam Dinh-Ninh Binh campaign in 1951 ; the Hoa Binh campaign in winter 1951 and spring 1952 ; the North-West campaign in winter 1952.

In these victorious campaigns, we put hundreds of thousands of enemy troops out of action and liberated vast areas in the mountainous regions of north Viet Nam. The important provinces on the Viet Nam-China border — Cao Bang, Lang Son, Lao Cai — the province of Hoa Binh on the road joining the Viet Bac to the Fourth zone, the great part of the North-West region from the Red River to the Viet Nam-Laos border, were successively liberated. Our rear was greatly expanded. In the mountainous regions of the north, the enemy occupied only Hai Ninh province in the North-East, and the town of Lai Chau and the fortified camp of Na San in the North-West.

While our main force scored successive victories on the main front, guerilla warfare strongly developed in all the areas behind the enemy's lines in north Viet Nam. Especially during the Hoa Binh campaign, our main force penetrated deep into the enemy rear on both sides of the

Red River, combined its action with the local armed and semi-armed forces, enlarged the guerilla bases and zones and freed millions of our compatriots. The temporarily occupied zones of the enemy were limited to only one third of the land and villages near the communication lines and important cities.

On the other fronts, in the enemy rear at Binh-Tri-Thien *, in the south of central Viet Nam and in Nam Bo, guerilla warfare was going on and developing, causing heavy losses to the enemy.

In summer 1953, the Pathet Lao forces, combined with the Viet Nam People's volunteers, launched a sudden attack on the town of Sam Neua. The bulk of the garrison was annihilated ; the town of Sam Neua and vast zones of Upper Laos were liberated, thus creating a new threat to the enemy.

Throughout north Viet Nam, we observed that from winter 1950 onwards, our forces constantly held the initiative in operations, driving the enemy more and more on to the defensive. To save this situation, the enemy made an urgent appeal to the American imperialists whose intervention in the aggressive war in Indo China had been constantly on the increase. During this period the French Government had several times changed the commanders of the French Expeditionary Corps. After the Border campaign, it sent to Indo-China the famous General de Lattre de Tassigny. As is known, Tassigny strove to concentrate his troops, fortify his defence lines, and launch an attack in the direction of

---

* Provinces in central Viet Nam Quang Binh Quang Tri. Thua Thien.

Hoa Binh in order to recapture the initiative in the operations, but he was finally defeated. His successor, **General Salan**, was, in his turn, an impotent witness to severe defeats of the Expeditionary Corps on the North-West and Upper Laos fronts

It was in this critical situation, that the American imperialists availed themvelves of the armistice in Korea to step up their intervention in Indo-China. And the " Navarre plan" expressed the new Franco-American scheme to prolong and extend the aggressive war in our country.

II — THE ENEMY'S NEW SCHEME
THE " NAVARRE PLAN "

In mid-1953, with the consent of Washington, the French Government appointed General Navarre Commander in-Chief of the French Expeditionary Corps in Indo-China.

Navarre and the French and American generals estimated that the more and more critical situation of the French Expeditionary Corps was due to the extreme dispersal of French forces in thousands of posts and garrisons scattered on all fronts to cope with our guerilla warfare ; as a result, they lacked a strong mobile force to face the attacks of our main force. During that time, our forces were constantly growing, our mobile forces increased day by day, the scale of our campaigns became larger and larger.

Basing themselves upon this estimation, Navarre and the French and American generals mapped out a plan to save the day, hoping to reverse the situation and to win, in a short period of time, a decisive strategic success.

The " Navarre plan" envisaged the organisation of a very strong strategic mobile force, capable of breaking all our offensives and annihilating the main part of our forces later on. For this purpose, Navarre ordered the regroupment of his picked European and African units, which were to be withdrawn from a number of posts. At the same time, new units from France, West Germany, North Africa and Korea were rushed to the Indo-China front.

In the carrying out of this plan, the enemy met a great contradiction, a serious difficulty : if they kept their forces scattered in order to occupy territory, it would be impossible for them to organise a strong mobile force; but if they reduced their occupation forces to regroup them, our guerillas would take advantage of the new weakness of their position to increase their activity, their posts and garrisons would be threatened or annihilated, the local puppet authorities overthrown, and the occupied zones reduced. Navarre sought to get round the difficulty by developing the puppet forces on a large scale to replace European and African troops transferred towards the re-grouping points. In fact, this treacherous idea was nothing new, and had already been applied by Tassigny. Faced with the new dangerous situation, Navarre and the French and American generals decided to organise ₃4 new battalions of puppet troops immediately and to double this number in the following year. Later on, the enemy had to acknowledge that this expedient did not help, because the increase in the puppet forces really only represented a quantitative increase at the expense of the quality of the units.

With their great mobile forces, the Franco-American imperialists conceived a rather audacious plan, aimed at

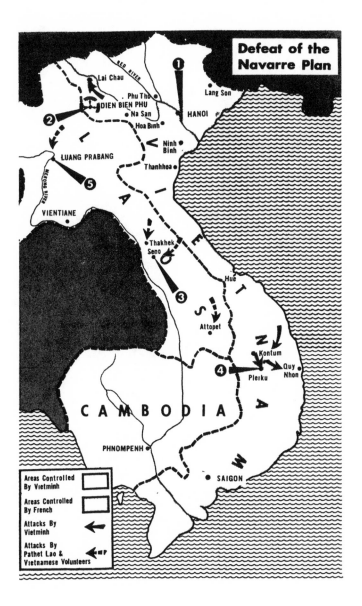

Defeat of the Navarre Plan

RED RIVER

Lai Chau

Phu Tho

DIEN BIEN PHU

Na San

Lang Son

HANOI

Hoa Binh

Ninh Binh

Thanhhoa

LUANG PRABANG

MEKONG RIVER

VIENTIANE

L A O S

Thakhek

Seno

Hue

Attopet

Kontum

Pleiku

Quy Nhon

V I E T N A M

C A M B O D I A

PHNOMPENH

SAIGON

Areas Controlled
By Vietminh

Areas Controlled
By French

Attacks By
Vietminh

Attacks By
Pathet Lao &
Vietnamese Volunteers

annihilating our main force and ending the war within 18 months.

On the one hand, they decided to concentrate their forces in the Red River delta in autumn and winter 1953 to open barbarous mopping-up operations to destroy our guerilla bases : on the other hand, they planned to launch attacks on our free zone in order to attract and exhaust our main forces. Simultaneously, they intended to create new battalions of puppet soldiers and re-group new units.

After winter, that is after the season of big operations in north Viet Nam, at the beginning of 1954, availing themselves of the fact that our army could at this time be resting, they would transfer to the south the greater part of their mobile forces. At this period, the climatic conditions in the south were favourable to their activity. Their intention was to open big operations to occupy all our free zones, particularly the Fifth and Ninth zones. To occupy all these regions would be for them tantamount to removing the gravest threats faced by them. Due to the impetus provided by these victories, they would recruit new puppet units, while continuing the regrouping of their mobile forces to prepare a decisive offensive on the front in the north.

If the plan were working well, in autumn and winter 1954, they would bring back to north Viet Nam their greatly increased forces, still under the influence of the enthusiasm created by their recent victories. In launching a major offensive against our bases, they would have occupied new territories, annihilated the bulk of our main forces to end the aggressive war and permanently transform the whole of Viet Nam into a colony and a Franco American military base.

According to his plan, in summer 1953, the enemy concentrated their forces. At the beginning of autumn, enemy mobile forces reached a total of 84 battalions in the whole of Indo-China.

To carry out the first phase of the " Navarre plan " the enemy concentrated in the Red River delta more than 50 per cent of their mobile forces, and declared that they were passing over to the offensive in order to regain the initiative in the operations. Scores of battalions launched savage mopping-up operations in the delta in order to consolidate the rear. Units of paratroops attacked Lang Son and it was announced that we had suffered heavy losses, although in fact our losses were insignificant. They launched a great attack on Nho Quan and on the region bordering Ninh Binh and Thanh Hoa provinces, and declared that the occupation of these provinces was imminent. But their troops had to withdraw with heavy losses.

In the North-West, the enemy withdraw from Na San to the delta. Formerly, Na San had been considered by them as " the second Verdun ", " blocking the road to the Southward advance of communism ", but when they had to evacuate it in order to escape destruction, they declared that Na San had lost all military interest. Before the evacuation, they saw that their myrmidons organised gangs of bandits in rather extensive areas to the north of this locality.

On November 20, 1953, the enemy dropped considerable paratroop forces into the valley of Dien Bien Phu. Their plan was to reinforce Dien Bien Phu, then go to Tuan Giao and Son La, re-occupy Na San and join it to Lai Chau. Thus Dien Bien Phu would become a strongpost threatening the flank of our North-West base. This new entrenched position would force us to scatter our troops between the delta and the mountains, and would protect

Upper Laos. It would constitute a spring-board for their next big offensive, one column pushing from the plain, the other from Dien Bien Phu to the delta. Thus, Dien Bien Phu became little by little a key position in the Navarre plan.

It was clear that in this autumn-winter period all enemy activities had one aim : to re-group forces, to strengthen the rear, to exhaust and scatter our forces, to prepare conditions for their coming great attacks They thought that the first phase of their plan had been successful when our Autumn-Winter campaign began.

III — OUR PLAN IN WINTER 1953 - SPRING 1954, AND THE EVOLUTION OF THE MILITARY SITUATION ON THE VARIOUS FRONTS

After the cease-fire in Korea, we anticipated that the new Franco-American scheme war to expand their forces and extend the aggressive war in Indo-China. Early in summer 1953, their military situation deteriorated. Taking advantage of the serious difficulties met by the French Expeditionary Corps following its successive defeats from 1950 onwards, the American imperialists intervened more openly and more actively in the war in Indo-China.

On our side, the army and people were transported with the impetus of the victorious big campaign ; guerilla warfare was developing in all regions under enemy control. Our army had accumulated more fighting experience, and its tactical and technical level had been raised through the summing-up of the experience of the military campaign and the training courses. Moreover, a new factor appeared this was the policy of systematic rent reduction, and the carrying out of land reform decided by the Party and Government. After the political course on the mobilisation of the peasant masses, our cadres and armymen saw more clearly that the objective of our struggle was : national independence, and land to the tillers. Hence, their combativeness increased greatly. More than ever our army was transported with enthusiasm, ready to go to the front to annihilate the enemy.

We were determined to break the " Navarre plan " and hold the new plot of the Franco-American imperialists in check. But how to do it ? Faced with the new difficulties, it was neccessary to analyse the situation to determine a correct line of action which ensured success.

The concrete problem was : the enemy was concentrating forces in the Red River delta, and launching attacks on our free zones. Now, had we to concentrate our forces to face the enemy, or to mobilise them for attacks in other directions ? The problem was difficult. In concentrating our forces to fight the enemy in the delta we could defend our free zone ; but here the enemy was still strong and we could easily be decimated. On the other hand, in attacking in other directions with our main forces, we could exploit the vulnerable points of the enemy to annihilate the bulk of their forces ; but our free zone would thus be threatened.

After a careful study of the situation, the Party's Central Committee issued the following slogan to break the " Navarre plan " : "dynamism, initiative, mobility, and rapidity of decision in face of new situations." Keeping the initiative, we should concentrate our forces to attack strategic points which were relatively vulnerable. If we succeeded in keeping the initiative, we could achieve successes and compel the enemy to scatter their forces, and finally, their plan to threaten our free zone could not be realised. On the other hand, if we were driven on to the defensive, not only could we not annihilate many enemy forces, but our own force could easily suffer losses, and, finally, it would be difficult for us to break the enemy threat.

On all fronts, our Winter-Spring plan was the expression of this strategic conception. In October 1953, hundreds of thousands of persons were mobilised to quicken the preparations. In mid-November, our main forces went to the front. The Winter-Spring campaign began.

Liberation of Lai Chau

On December 10, 1953, we opened fire on the Lai Chau front. Formerly, we had annihilated or forced to surrender thousands of bandits in the regions of Muong La and Chau Thuan. On that very night, we wiped out the outpost of Paham, about 30 kilometres from Lai Chau Aware of the presence of our main forces, the enemy was very afraid and ordered the garrison to withdraw from Lai Chau and to rally to Dien Bien Phu by the mountain tracks.

Our troops were ordered to march on to liberate Lai Chau, while one column attacked westward, cutting off the enemy's retreat to encircle and annihilate him.

On December 12, Lai Chau was liberated.

On December 13, we annihilated the enemy in retreat at Muong Pon. After ten days and ten nights of fighting, pursuit and encirclement in a mountainous region, we liberated the remaining part of the zone occupied by the enemy in Lai Chau province. The enemy lost 24 companies.

It was the first great success of our Winter-Spring campaign. It strengthened the faith of our army and people. Moreover, it obliged the enemy to send reinforcements to Dien Bien Phu. It was the first miscarriage of Navarre's regrouping plan. Our troops began to encircle the fortified entrenched camp of Dien Bien Phu.

Liberation of Thakhek and several regions in Middle Laos

Parallel with the preparations to attack Lai Chau orders were given to the Viet Nam People's volunteers to cooperate with the Pathet Lao troops to launch an offensive on the Middle Laos front, where the enemy was relatively vulnerable. At the beginning of December, the enemy became aware of our activity, and quickly rushed reinforcements to this sector. On December 22, the Vietnamese and Laotian units carried by storm the post of Banaphao, a strong entrenched position which controlled the frontier. Other units struck deep into the enemy's rear. After a series of victories, the Vietnamese and Laotian units made very quick progress towards Thakhek, at the same time pursuing the enemy in his flight along Road No. 9.

Bewildered, the enemy withdrew from Thakhek to Seno, a military base near Savannakhet, losing on the way three battalions of infantry and one artillery unit. On December 27, the Pathet Lao units and the Viet Nam People's volunteers entered Thakhek, and reached the bank of the Mekong. The liberated zones were extended to Road No. 9.

This was the second important victory in the Winter-Spring campaign. To face our activity in time, the enemy had to withdraw mobile forces from the Red River delta and from the South, to send them to Seno. To impede the Vietnamese and Laotian units in an advance into Lower Laos, they strengthened this base. Navarre was obliged to scatter his forces over several points.

Liberation of the Bolovens Highland and the town of Attopeu

Simultaneously with the attack on the Middle Laos front, one unit of the Laotian and Vietnamese forces crossed dangerous mountainous regions, and advanced into Lower Laos where it effected a junction with local armed forces.

On December 30 and 31, the Laotian and Vietnamese units defeated an enemy battalion in the region of Attopeu and liberated this town. Exploiting their victory, they advanced towards Saravane, and liberated the whole Bolovens Highland to south of Road No. 9. The enemy had to send reinforcements to Pakse.

Liberation of Kontum and the north of the Western Highlands of central Viet Nam

In spite of defeats at various points, the enemy remained subjective in making estimations. Due to the easy occupation of Dien Bien Phu, the enemy thought we were incapable of attacking it. According to them, the entrenched camp was too strong for our troops. Moreover they thought that the distance which separated it from our rear created insuperable obstacles for us in the supply of food. They thought we had passed to the attack at different points because we did not know how to deal with Dien Bien Phu; they thought that shortly, we should be obliged to evacuate the North-West because of supply difficulties; then they would find the means to destroy a part of our main forces and would continue execution of their plan: the occupation of Tuan Giao and Son La and the return to Na San.

It was this same subjective estimation which made them launch the Atlanta operation against the south of Phu Yen in the Fifth zone. This well-prepared attack was the first step in the occupation of our whole free zone in the south of central Viet Nam, as foreseen by the "Navarre plan".

Our strategic principle was: "dynamism, initiative." Our troops in the Fifth zone received the order to leave behind only a small part of their forces to cope with the enemy, while the bulk would continue their regroupment and pass to the offensive in the north of the Western Highlands. We opened the campaign on January 26. The following day, we took the Mandel sub-sector, the strongest sub-sector of the enemy. The post of Dakto was taken and we liberated the whole north of Kontum province. On February 17, we liberated the town of Kontum, wiped out the enemy in the whole north of the Western Highlands, and advanced as far as Road No. 19. Meanwhile, we attacked Pleiku. The enemy was at a loss, and had to stop the offensive in the coastal plains of the Fifth zone and withdraw many units from Middle Laos and the three Vietnamese provinces of Quang Binh, Quang Tri and Thua Thien to reinforce the Western Highlands.

This was another victory for our forces in the Winter-Spring campaign. It proved once more the correctness of the guiding principle of the Central Committee. The enemy was more and more obviously driven on to the defensive. They had to mobilise forces from the Red River delta to reinforce Middle Laos, and afterwards from Middle Laos to reinforce the Western Highlands. They had concentrated forces to make a lightning offensive against our Fifth zone but had to stop their action in order to protect themselves against our blows.

Our offensive on the Western Highlands was victoriously carried on till June 1954, and scored many more successes, particularly the resounding victory at An Khe where we cut to pieces the mobile regiment No. 100 which had just returned from Korea, thus liberating An Khe. Our troops captured in this battle a large number of vehicles and a great quantity of ammunition.

Liberation of Phong Saly and the Nam Hu river basin, the push forward towards Luang Prabang

Dien Bien Phu was encircled after the defeat of Lai Chau. The French High Command tried to effect junction between the Dien Bien Phu entrenched camp and Upper Laos by increasing their occupation forces along the Nam Hu river basin as far as Muong Khoa, intending to establish liaison with Dien Bien Phu.

To put them on the wrong track, to annihilate more of their forces, to weaken them more, and oblige them to continue to scatter their troops in order to create favourable conditions for our preparations at Dien Bien Phu, orders were given to our units to combine with the Pathet Lao forces to launch an offensive in the Nam Hu river basin.

On January 26, the Vietnamese and Laotian forces attacked Muong Khoa where they destroyed one European regiment; then, exploiting this success, they wiped out the enemy in the Nam Hu river basin, and came within striking distance of Luang Prabang, while one column pushed northward and liberated Phong Saly.

Before our strong offensive, the enemy had to withdraw mobile units from the Red River delta to send them to Upper Laos. Thus, Navarre was obliged to scatter his forces still further.

Our successes in the enemy rear in the Red River delta, the three provinces of Quang Binh, Quang Tri, Thua Thien, and Nam Bo

While the enemy was in difficulties on all fronts, our local armed forces, people's militia and guerillas effectively exploited the situation in the enemy rear and strongly combined activity with the front.

In the Red River delta, a series of enemy fortified camps was destroyed; and Road No. 5 was seriously threatened, being sometimes cut for weeks together. In two great attacks on Cat Bi (March 7, 1954) and Gia Lam airfields (March 8, 1954) our armymen destroyed 78 enemy planes.

At Binh-Tri-Thien, and in the southernmost part of central Viet Nam, our armymen's activity was intense; they expanded the guerilla bases, increased propaganda work directed to the enemy and won many successes.

In Nam Bo, through the whole winter-spring period, our armymen pushed forward their combined action, and obtained very great successes: more than one hundred enemy posts and watch-towers were either destroyed or evacuated, many localities were liberated, and the number of soldiers crossing to our side amounted to several thousands.

The development of hostilities until March 1954 showed that to a great extent the " Navarre plan " had collapsed. The enemy's plan to concentrate was essentially foiled. At this moment, enemy mobile forces were no longer concentrated in the Red River delta; they were scattered over several points: Luang Prabang and Muong Sai in Upper Laos, Seno in Middle Laos, the south of the Western Highlands in the Fifth zone, and large forces were pinned down at Dien Bien Phu. In the Red River delta, what was left of their mobile forces amounted to only 20 regiments, but a great part of these forces was no longer mobile and had to be scattered in order to protect the communication lines, particularly Road No. 5.

The situation of hostilities developed contrary to the enemy's will.

Navarre intended to concentrate his forces in the Red River delta with a view to recovering the initiative, but we obliged him to scatter his forces everywhere and passively take measures to protect himself.

He intended to annihilate a part of our main forces, but it was not our main forces but his that suffered heavy losses. He intended to attack our free zone, but instead his rear was severely attacked by us. Thus we threatened his whole system of disposition of forces.

However, the Franco-American generals did not want to recognise this disastrous truth. They still thought our activity in winter 1953-spring 1954 had reached its peak, that our withdrawal was beginning, that we lacked the strength to continue our activity, and that their favourable moment was approaching.

As a result, in order to get back the initiative, on March 12, the enemy resumed the Atlanta plan which had been interrupted, and opened an attack by landing at Quy Nhon.

Not for a moment did they believe that on the following day, March 13, 1954, we would launch a large-scale attack on the Dien Bien Phu entrenched camp. Thus, the historic Dien Bien Phu Campaign began.

IV — THE HISTORIC
DIEN BIEN PHU CAMPAIGN

Dien Bien Phu is a large plain 18 kilometres long and six to eight kilometres wide in the mountainous zone of the North-West. It is the biggest and richest of the four plains in this hilly region close to the Viet Nam-Laos frontier. It is situated at the junction of important roads, running to the North-East towards Lai Chau, to the East and South-East towards Tuan Giao, Son La, Na San; to the West towards Luang Prabang and to the South towards Sam Neua. In the theatre of operations of Bac Bo and Upper Laos, Dien Bien Phu is a strategic position of first importance, capable of becoming an infantry and air base of extreme efficiency.

At the beginning there were at Dien Bien Phu only ten enemy battalions but they were gradually reinforced to cope with our offensive. When we launched the attack, the enemy forces totalled 17 battalions and 10 companies, comprising chiefly Europeans and Africans and units of highly-trained paratroops. Moreover the camp had three battalions of artillery, one battalion of sappers, one armoured company, a transport unit of 200 lorries and a permanent squadron of 12 aircraft. Altogether 16,200 men.

The forces were distributed in three sub-sectors which had to support one another and comprised 49 strong-points. Each had defensive autonomy, several were grouped in " complex defence centres " equipped with mobile forces and artillery, and surrounded by trenches and barbed wire, hundreds of metres thick. Each sub-sector comprised several strongly fortified defence centres.

But the most important was the Central sub-sector situated in the middle of the Muong Thanh village, the chief town of Dien Bien Phu. Two-thirds of the forces of the garrison were concentrated here. It had several connected defence centres protecting the command post, the artillery and commissariat bases, and at the same time the airfield. To the East, well-situated hills formed the most important defence system of the sub-sector, Dien Bien Phu was considered by the enemy to be an unassailable and impregnable fortress.

In fact, the central sub-sector did have rather strong forces, and the heights in the East could not be attacked easily. Besides, the artillery and armoured forces could break every attempt at intervention through the plain, a system of barbed wire and trenches would permit the enemy to decimate and repel any assault, and the mobile forces formed by the battalions of paratroops, whose action was combined with that of the defence centres, could counter-attack and break any offensive. The Northern sub-sector comprised the defence centres of Him Lam, Doc Lap and Ban Keo. The very strong positions of Him Lam and Doc Lap were required to check all attacks of our troops coming from Tuan Giao and Lai Chau.

As for the Southern sub-sector, also known as Hong Cum sub-sector, its purpose was to break any offensive coming from the South and to protect the communication way with Upper Laos.

Their artillery was divided between two bases : one at Muong Thanh, the other at Hong Cum, arranged in such a way as to support each other and to support all the surrounding strong-points.

Dien Bien Phu had two airfields : besides the main field at Muong Thanh, there was a reserve field at Hong Cum ; they linked with Hanoi and Haiphong in an airlift which ensured 70 to 80 transports of supply daily.

The reconnaissance planes and fighters of the permanent squadron constantly flew over the entire region. The planes from the Gia Lam and Cat Bi airbases had the task of strafing and bombing our army. Navarre asserted that with such powerful forces and so strong a defence system, Dien Bien Phu was " an impregnable fortress... " The American general O'Daniel who paid a visit to the base shared this opinion. From this subjective point of view the enemy came to the conclusion that our troops had little chance in an attack on Dien Bien Phu. They even considered that an attack on our part would be a good opportunity for them to inflict a defeat on us.

On our side, after the liberation of Lai Chau, the attack upon Dien Bien Phu was on the agenda. We considered that the base, well entrenched as it was, also had vulnerable points. In attacking it, we faced difficulties in strategy, tactics and supply; but these difficulties could be overcome. After having analysed the situation, and weighed the pros and cons, we decided to attack Dien Bien Phu according to the method : to take no risks. Our tactic would be to attack each enemy defence centre, each part of the entrenched camp, thus creating conditions for the launching of a general offensive to annihilate the whole camp.

Three months had passed from the occupation of Dien Bien Phu enemy paratroops to the launching of our campaign. During that time, the enemy did their utmost to consolidate their defence system, gather reinforcements, dig new trenches, and strengthen their entrenchments.

On our side, the army and people actively prepared the offensive, carrying out the orders of the Party's Central Committee and the Government; the army and people mustered all their strength to guarantee the success of the Winter-Spring campaign, to which Dien Bien Phu was the key. Our troops succeeded in liberating the surrounding regions, isolating Dien Bien Phu, obliging the enemy to scatter forces and thus reduce their possibilities of sending reinforcements to the battlefield. We made motor roads, cleared the tracks to haul up artillery pieces, built casemates, for the artillery, prepared the ground for the offensive and encirclement ; in short, transformed the relief of the battlefield terrain with a view to solving the tactical problems. We overcame very great difficulties. We called upon our local compatriots to supply food, to set up supply lines hundreds of kilometres long from Thanh Hoa or Phu Tho to the North-West, crossing very dangerous areas and very high hills. We used every means to carry food and ammunition to the front. Our troops and voluntary workers ceaselessly went to the front and actively participated in the preparations under the bombs and bullets of enemy aircraft.

In the first week of March, the preparations were completed : the artillery had solid casemates, the operational bases were established, food and ammunition were available in sufficient quantity. After having been educated in the aim and significance of the campaign, all officers and soldiers were filled with a very high determination to annihilate the enemy, as they were persuaded that only the destruction of the Dien Bien Phu entrenched camp would bring the " Navarre plan " to complete failure.

On March 13, 1954, our troops received the order to launch an offensive against Dien Bien Phu.

The campaign proceeded in three phases: in the first phase we destroyed the Northern sub-sector; in the second, the longest and bitterest one, we took the heights in the East of the Central sub-sector and tightened our encirclement; in the third, we launched the general offensive and annihilated the enemy.

First phase : destruction of Northern sub-sector

This phase began on March 13th and ended on March 17th. On the night of March 13th, we annihilated the very strong defence centre of Him Lam which overlooked the road from Tuan Giao to Dien Bien Phu. The battle was very sharp, the enemy artillery concentrated its fire, and poured scores of thousands of shells on our assaulting waves. Our troops carried the position in the night. This first victory had very deep repercussions on the development of the whole campaign.

In the night of the 14th, we concentrated our forces to attack the defence centre of Doc Lap, the second strong defence sector of the Northern sub sector which overlooked the road from Lai Chau to Dien Bien Phu. The battle went on till dawn. The enemy used every means to repel our forces, fired scores of thousands of shells and sent their mobile forces protected by tanks from Muong Thanh to support their position. Our troops fought heroically, took the strong-point and repelled the enemy reinforcements.

The third and last defence centre of the Northern sub-sector, the Ban Keo post, became isolated and was threatened by us. This was a less strong position, manned by a garrison chiefly made up of puppet soldiers. On March 17th, the whole garrison left its positions and surrendered. After the loss of the Northern sub-sector, the Central sub-sector, now exposed on its eastern, northern flanks, was threatened.

In the fighting in the first phase, the correctness of our tactical decisions, the good organisation of our defence and anti-aircraft activity reduced the efficiency of the enemy artillery and air force. Besides, our artillery fire, which was very accurate, inflicted heavy losses on the enemy. The main airfield was threatened. Our anti-aircraft batteries went into action for the first time and brought down enemy planes. But above all, it was by their heroic spirit, their high spirit of sacrifice and their will to win, that our troops distinguished themselves during these battles.

The great and resounding victory which ended the first phase of operations stirred our army and people and gave each and every one faith in final victory.

As for the enemy, despite their heavy losses, they still had confidence in the power of resistance of the Central sub-sector, in the strength of their artillery and air force. They even expected that we would suffer heavy losses and would be obliged to give up the offensive; and especially, that if the campaign was protected our supply lines would be cut and that the great logistic difficulties thus created would force us to withdraw.

Second phase: Occupation of the hills in the East and encirclement of the Central sub-sector

The second phase was the most important of the campaign. We had to deal with the Central sub-sector, in the middle of the Muong Thanh plain, and new difficulties arose in the conduct of the operations. Our troops had to work actively to complete the operations; they had to dig a vast network of trenches, from the neighbouring hills to the plain, to encircle the Central sub-sector and cut it off from the Southern sector. This advance of our lines which encircled the enemy positions was made at the cost of fierce fighting. By every means the enemy tried to upset our preparations by the fire of their air force and artillery. However, our troops drew closer to their positions with irresistible power in the course of uninterrupted fighting.

During the night of March 30th, the second phase began. We launched a large scale attack of long duration to annihilate the heights in the East and a certain number of strong-points in the West in order to tighten our encirclement, and to hamper and cut off the supplies to the garrison. On this night of March 30th, we concentrated important forces to attack simultaneously the five fortified heights in the East. On this same night, we succeeded in capturing hills E-1, D-1 and C-1, but could not take hill

A-1, the most important of all. The defence line constituted by these heights was the key to the defensive system of the Central sub-sector: its loss would lead to the fall of Dien Bien Phu. Consequently, the fight here was at its fiercest. Particularly on hill A-1, the last height which protected the commant post, the battle lasted until April 4th. Every inch of ground was hotly disputed. Finally, we occupied half of the position while the enemy, entrenched in casemates and trenches, continued to resist in the other half. While this fighting was going on, the garrison received paratroop reinforcements.

On April 9th, the enemy launched a counter-attack to re-occupy hill C-1. The battle went on for four days and nights, and the position was occupied half by the enemy and half by us.

While the situation in the East was static, in the North and in the West our encirclement grew tighter and tighter. The lines of both sides drew nearer and nearer, in some points they were only 10 to 15 metres away from each other. From the occupied positions to the battlefields northward and westward, the fire of our artillery and mortars pounded the enemy without let-up. Day and night the fighting went on. We exhausted the enemy by harassing them, firing constantly at their lines, and at the same time tried to take their strong points one by one with a tactic of combined nibbling advance and full scale attack.

In mid-April, after the destruction of several enemy positions in the North and West, our lines reached the airfield, then cut it from West to East. Our encirclement grew still tighter, the fighting was still more fierce. The enemy launched several violent counter-attacks supported by tanks and aircraft aimed at taking ground from us and obliging us to loosen our encirclement. On April 24th, the most violent counter-attack was launched with the aim of driving us off the airfield : after inflicting heavy losses on the enemy, we remained the master, and the airfield stayed in our control.

The territory occupied by the enemy shrank in size day by day, and they were driven into a two kilometres square. It was threatened by our heavy fire. The enemy's supply problem became more and more critical. The airfield had been out of action for a long time, all supplies were being dropped by parachute. But as the enemy zone was so narrow, and their pilots feared our anti-aircraft fire and dared not fly low, only a part of the parachutes carrying food and ammunition fell into the enemy position, and the bulk of them fell on our ground ; thus we poured shells parachuted by the enemy on the entrenched camp.

Throughout the second phase, the situation was extremely tense. The American interventionists sent more bombers and transport planes to support the Dien Bien Phu base. The enemy bombers were very active ; they ceaselessly bombed our positions, dropped napalm bombs to burn down the vegetation on the heights surrounding Dien Bien Phu, and bombed points that they took for our artillery bases. Day and night they shelled our supply lines, dropped blockbusters on the roads, showered the roads with delayed action and " butterfly " bombs, in an endeavour to cut our supply lines. These desperate efforts did not achieve the desired results. They could not check the flow of hundreds of thousands of voluntary workers, pack-horses and transport cars carrying food and ammunition to the front. They could not stop us from carrying out our plan of encirclement, the condition of their destruction.

The French and American generals clearly saw the danger of the destruction of the Dien Bien Phu entrenched camp.

At this moment, the High Command of the French Expeditionary Corps thought of gathering together the remaining forces for an attack on our rear and in the direction of the Viet Bac, to cut our supply lines and oblige us to withdraw for lack of food and ammunition. But it could not carry out this plan. Moreover, it feared that a still more severe defeat could be the result of so foolhardy an action. At another time it intended to regroup the Dien Bien Phu garrison in several columns which would try to break through our encirclement and open at all costs a way towards Upper Laos. Finally, it had to give up this plan and continue to defend its positions.

Third phase : Annihilation of the enemy

On May 1st, began the third phase. From May 1st to May 6th, following several successive attacks, we occupied hill C-1, hill A-1 which was the key of the last defensive system of the Central sub sector, and several other strongpoints from the foot of the hills in the East to the Nam Gion river, and, finally some positions in the West.

The enemy was driven into a square kilometre, entirely exposed to our fire. There was no fortified height to protect them. The problem of supply became very grave. Their situation was critical : the last hour of the entrenched camp had come.

In the afternoon of May 7th, from the East and West, we launched a massive combined attack upon the headquarters at Muong Thanh. At several posts, the enemy hoisted the white flag and surrendered. At 5.30 p.m. we seized the headquarters : General de Castries and his staff were captured.

The remaining forces at Dien Bien Phu surrendered. The prisoners of war were well treated by our troops.

The " Determined to fight and to win " banner of our army fluttered high in the valley of Dien Bien Phu. On this very night, we attacked the South sub-sector. The whole garrison of more than 2,000 men was captured.

The historic Dien Bien Phu campaign ended in our complete victory. Our troops had fought with an unprecedented heroism for 55 days and 55 nights.

During this time, our troops were very active in all theatres of operation in co-ordination with the main front.

In the enemy rear in the Red River delta, they destroyed, one after another, a large number of positions and seriously threatened road No. 5.

In the Fifth zone, they attacked road No. 19, annihilated the mobile regiment No. 100, liberated An Khe, penetrated deep into the region of Cheo Reo, and threatened Pleiku and Banmethuot.

Our troops were also very active in the region of Hue and in Nam Bo.

In Middle Laos, the Vietnamese and Laotian units increased their activity on road No. 9 and advanced southward.

Our troops won victories on all fronts.

*   *

Such are the broad outlines of the military situation in Winter 1953 and Spring 1954.

On all fronts, we put out of action 112,000 enemy troops and brought down or destroyed on the ground 177 planes.

At Dien Bien Phu, we put out of action 16,200 enemy troops, including the whole staff of the entrenched camp, one general, 16 colonels, 1,749 officers and warrant-officers, brought down or destroyed 62 planes of all types, seized all the enemy's armaments, ammunition and equipment, and more than 30,000 parachutes.

These great victories of the Viet Nam People's Army and people as a whole at Dien Bien Phu and on the other fronts had smashed to pieces the " Navarre plan ", and impeded the attempts of the Franco-American imperialists to prolong and extend the war These great victories liberated the North of Viet Nam, contributed to the success of the Geneva Conference and the restoration of peace in Indo-China on the basis of respect of the sovereignty, independence, national unity and territorial integrity of Viet Nam and of the two friendly countries, Cambodia and Laos.

These are glorious pages of our history, of our People's Army and our people. They illustrate the striking success of our Party in leading the movement for national liberation against the French imperialists and the American interventionists.